Getting Help

A Woman's Guide to Therapy

Getting Help

A Woman's Guide to Therapy

Elizabeth Robson & Gwenyth Edwards

E. P. DUTTON | NEW YORK

For information contact:
E.P. Dutton, 2 Park Avenue, New York, N.Y. 10016

Library of Congress Cataloging in Publication Data
Robson, Elizabeth.
Getting help: a woman's guide to therapy.
Bibliography: p.   1. Psychotherapy.   2. Psychotherapists.   3. Women
—Mental health.   4. Consumer education.   I. Edwards, Gwenyth, joint
author.   II. Title.   RC480.5.R57   616.8'914   79-22086

ISBN: 0-525-93061-2 (cloth)
ISBN: 0-525-93117-1 (paper)

Published simultaneously in Canada by Clarke, Irwin & Company
Limited, Toronto and Vancouver

Designed by Barbara Huntley

10 9 8 7 6 5 4 3 2 1

First Edition

In memory of Pat Klein

Contents

The Therapy Contract
Confidentiality
Feelings
Termination

Giving and Receiving Criticism or Feedback
Minor Complaints
Major Complaints

Why Are Women Hospitalized?
Types of Mental Hospitals
How Do You Get In?
How Do You Get Out?
Alternatives to Hospitalization
Recommended Readings on Hospitalization

Referral Sources
Types of Mental Health Services and How to Find Them

Acknowledgments

We would like to thank our husbands, Lee Goldstein and Roland Mattison, for the time and effort they put into such tasks as child care, editing, Xeroxing, and collating. Thanks also to our editors: Nancy Crawford, who worked with us to develop the idea, Connie Schrader, and Julie Coryn. Finally, our appreciation goes to all the women who took the time to fill out the questionnaires.

Preface

It seems you can't walk into a bookstore nowadays without seeing a new book about therapy. While some are the usual technical books meant for the therapist, there are also dozens of self-help books offering people new ways to improve their lives. Knowing that many women do not have the time or energy to wade through technical books which may be written in obscure language (and which often do not speak to their concerns), and further realizing that the self-help books are no help to the women who want the help of an experienced therapist, we have taken on the task of writing a guide for the woman consumer that will help her select an effective therapist and get the most out of therapy.

We have a long-standing commitment to consumer education in the area of mental health services. We, along with Sheryll Bloom, Dayl Cohen, Denise Curran, Pat Klein, and Marla Zarrow, published a short booklet in 1975 entitled *Off the Couch.* This was a project of the Women and Therapy Collective of the Goddard/Cambridge Graduate Program in Social Change (now defunct), of which we were all members. The booklet was an effort to reach women who were considering therapy, and to provide them with some guidelines for choosing a therapist. Our present work is an expansion of that concept and reflects our thinking, both as therapists and as one-time clients who wish we had had this information when looking for therapy some years ago. We see this book as an attempt to educate the consumer of therapy services to look after her own interests (in the process strengthening her ability to do so) and to demystify the therapy process. We think this book will be valuable not only to the woman currently considering therapy, but to the woman already in therapy, as a guide to evaluating and understanding her experience.

Before writing this book, we sent out questionnaires to women all over the country, asking them to share their experience of therapy with us. This was not a formal study, and we made no formal analysis of the results. Instead, it was simply an opportunity for women to say in their own words what therapy was like for them and to tell us what they consider important in a therapy relationship. We have included quotes from many of these questionnaires and from personal interviews throughout the book when they are pertinent to what we are discussing. We feel that "hearing" the voices of women describing their own therapy experiences will be helpful to the reader who is trying to imagine what therapy is really like.

Besides including the "voices" and words of women, we have tried to make this book belong to women in another, vital way. We know that language is important, and written language has a strong effect on our ability to conceptualize ideas. Some recent books have asserted that their use of the masculine pronoun, or of words like *mankind,* is only for convenience and of course refers as well to women. There is no way to minimize the effect on women of always reading *he* in books and having to supply the invisible she. We have tried to remedy this by using the somewhat awkward *s/he* or *her/him* when referring to therapists, since they may be either male or female. Because this book is addressed specifically to women, we have used *she* or *her* to refer to the client. We have also used the word *therapist* throughout the book even though in many places *counselor, psychologist,* or any of the other specific titles might have been used. We use the term *client* because it means a person who is buying professional services. In the discussion of some schools of therapy, we have used the term *patient* only because it is always used by practitioners of those particular schools. In general, we do not approve of the term *patient* because it means someone who is sick.

The book is divided into three major sections. Part I introduces the reader to the subject of women's special needs in psychotherapy and to how the Women's Movement has made women consumers more aware of the problems and prejudices facing them in the selection of a therapist. Part II describes the major schools of therapy in this country and evaluates them from the point of view of women's needs. Part III is a guide to practical considerations involved in interviewing and selecting a therapist and in the ongoing relationship with that person.

Women have been working very hard to reclaim control over their own bodies and secure the right to adequate health care. They have also been working to eliminate sexist discrimination in all areas of their lives. Psychotherapy as a profession has been delinquent in both respects. We hope this book contributes to the process of proving therapy to be something of value to any woman who chooses to use it.

Part
I
Women
and Therapy

Chapter

1

Thinking about Therapy

If you are reading this book, you are probably thinking about seeing a psychotherapist or you are in therapy now. And you are not at all unusual. Statistics show that women are by far the major consumers of mental health care. Today more women than ever before are entering therapy and talking about it, whereas until recently they have been reluctant to do both. This reluctance has stemmed for the most part from the stigma most people have attached to the process of seeing a therapist ("If you go to a 'shrink' you must be crazy").

Why are women's attitudes toward therapy changing? The answers are complex. Interpersonal difficulties, marital and family crises, and the anxiety and depression that accompany such problems are still the most common reasons for seeking the help of a therapist. Yet more and more women are now viewing therapy as a tool to help them deal with the vast changes in role and lifestyle so many of us are experiencing today.

The Women's Movement is an obvious cause of the

3

change of attitude toward woman's traditional role as wife and mother. The new opportunities we have created for ourselves outside the home have been both exciting and a source of pain and anxiety for many of us. Therapy for women today is often viewed as a means to grow as an individual by learning how to handle these changes in a personally satisfying way.

Most women know very little about how therapy works, even when they are in therapy. But with the ever-increasing numbers of women seeing therapists, more are realizing the need to educate themselves about this seemingly mysterious process. The more you know about therapy, the more you can see that it is not some kind of magical process that will transform you or force you to change against your will, but is really a way of gaining a broader perspective on your life.

This book is intended to help you—a prospective client in psychotherapy—to answer the questions you may have about therapy, to explain clearly the theories and procedures so you know what to expect, and to help you make your therapy a rewarding experience. If you are already in therapy, our intention is to help you understand what is happening and why yours is or is not an effective therapy relationship.

What Is Psychotherapy?

The term *psychotherapy* describes any of a broad range of services designed to treat mental or emotional problems. The primary function of therapy is to help you understand yourself and the problems you face in your life so that you can handle those problems rather than be overwhelmed by them. How this is effected is through a process of self-confrontation, understanding, and ultimately, change. You can change when you are finally able to talk with a therapist, in an atmosphere of interest, warmth and tolerance, about what troubles you.

There are many schools of therapy, and each school develops its own theory of how the mind works, how problems develop, and how these problems should be treated. Choosing a therapist from such a conglomeration of treatment philosophies can be very confusing when you are looking for help. However, despite the multiplicity of theories of psychotherapy, there are some common characteristics of good therapists and good therapy which you can keep in mind and which we will be discussing throughout this book.

Because of the domination of the field by psychiatrists (all of whom are M.D.'s), many women feel psychotherapy is a medical treatment prescribed for a specific ailment in the same way, for instance, that a doctor prescribes penicillin for strep throat. Psychotherapy is *not* a medical treatment (although drugs are often used in conjunction with therapy). We believe that treating emotional problems as an illness to be cured is a harmful rather than helpful approach. It negates your responsibility for understanding what is wrong in your life and working on it, and it encourages the mystification of the therapeutic process by implying that therapy is a technical skill acquired only by many years of study in medical school. Instead, therapy should provide you with an opportunity to discuss problems and alternatives with someone who is not involved in your daily life, someone who can be a sounding board for your feelings and help you clarify your situation. It can be a chance to talk about things you do not feel comfortable discussing with friends or relatives. The support of your therapist may provide you with the strength you need to cope with and try to change unsatisfactory conditions in your life.

What Therapy Can Do for You

Therapy will not necessarily solve all your problems, but it should help you understand what those problems are.

Therapy has effectively helped women resolve a wide variety of personal difficulties, including depression, psychosomatic illnesses, drug addiction, phobias, excessive bereavement, and troubles with personal relationships. You will also learn skills such as decision-making, relaxation, or assertiveness training, all of which can help you handle stress. The more effective you are in dealing with your life, the stronger and more confident you will feel about yourself as a person.

Your therapist should be able to help you understand when your problems result from true internal conflicts and when they result from your social conditioning as a woman. Negative social attitudes toward women as a group often show up in an individual's lack of self-esteem, for example. Feminine traits (e.g., emotional, sensitive, or nurturing) are not as highly-valued socially as are so-called masculine traits (e.g., aggressiveness, rationality, objectivity), and as a result, women have a more negative self-image than men. Therapy should help you learn how your concept of femininity has been limiting or destructive to you, and where you can explore alternatives to women's traditional role in order to find what suits you best as an individual.

Individual and social problems overlap for many women who come to therapy. Some of these special situations that can be helped by therapy include rape, incest, and battering. Statistics show, for example, that in the United States one out of every four girls is sexually abused before she reaches the age of eighteen. While it is frequently assumed her assailant is a stranger, in 75 percent of the cases the victim knows her assailant. In 34 percent of the cases the molestation takes place in her home. Legal experts think that wife abuse is one of the most under-reported crimes in the country—even more so than rape, which the FBI estimates is ten times more frequent than statistics indicate. A conservative estimate puts the number of battered wives nationwide at well over a million.

Effective therapy is *not* BAND-AID treatment. Growth for women will at times involve pain and anger, but these feelings are not necessarily bad if they are healthy reactions to an unhealthy environment. Eliminating your anger or alleviating your pain may merely be a way of adjusting to a bad situation rather than allowing yourself to grow as a person. As one woman reports, "I thought therapy would help me feel less anger. It hasn't—it just helps me put the anger in constructive places."

Problems That Bring Women to Therapy

Most women who come to therapy are depressed or anxious, often without knowing why and without knowing what to do about it. The National Institute of Mental Health (NIMH) warns that one out of five women can expect to be clinically depressed (incapacitated to some degree by depression; i.e., not able to function in her usual role) in her lifetime. And depression, the nation's number-one mental health problem, occurs in women in a ratio of three-to-one as compared with men. While each individual must deal with her own particular background and set of circumstances, there are certain problems that all women face simply because we are women.

As women, we have learned to identify ourselves through our relationships rather than through our work or independent accomplishments. Instead of beautician or lawyer, we are more likely to think of ourselves as "John's wife" or "Suzy's mother." We often spend our lives taking care of other people's needs and ignoring our own; we think standing up for ourselves is selfish or unladylike. And for all our efforts, we end up with a vague self-image, little self-confidence, and almost no self-esteem. Those women who do value work equally with relationships are often punished: they might be excluded from social life for being "too smart" or shunned by men for being "castrating bitches." Women who do not have a relationship with a man, or who take on roles not considered feminine, are often derogatorily referred to as "butches" or "dykes."

Today, however, women are facing the greatest upheaval of roles in history. Western society has changed more in this century as a result of technology than it has in all the preceding centuries together. We, as women, have seen our parents divorcing, our friends leaving husband and children for something "more fulfilling," our sisters rejecting relationships with men entirely, our daughters rejecting us. How have these changes affected us as individuals?

At times we might wonder who we are and where we fit in. If we go to work, what have we lost in the home? If we stay at home, who will accuse us of talents gone to waste? What will we do with the empty years that stretch ahead when the children have grown and left home? If we have both a family and a job, have we enough strength to cope with it all? If the choices are still ahead of us, what resources do we have to draw on to act in our own best interests? Who are our models? Our mothers? It's the rare woman nowadays who feels she would like to live her life the way her mother did. Today's society—transient, disconnected, fast-moving—demands that each of us be self-reliant and resourceful. Depending on some authority to tell you how to live your life, whether that authority be parents, husband, or the church, is no longer practical or possible, let alone desirable. Many women therefore come to therapy to learn how to gain confidence in themselves and be responsible for their own lives.

Woman's Changing Role—Myth and Reality

Options available to younger women disappear as those women reach middle and old age. The reality is that although much has changed, women must continue to struggle to retain what we have and to attain equal status with men as first-class citizens. Older women face a greater struggle against sex-role stereotypes because they have lived with them longer and have tended to structure their lives around this identity.

Women now live an average of three decades beyond the childbearing years. What we do with our lives after age forty-five is a question that much of society seems indifferent to. We need to redefine our roles in middle age, and these changes need to be supported, but finding that support can be a difficult task. The woman who is divorced in her forties, for example, after spending the previous twenty-five years in the home, will probably have to face the prospect of reentering the job market with no training and few marketable skills, at the same time competing with women fresh out of college. This can be a devastating experience, and helpful resources are not always available.

In this society there is a double standard applied to the process of aging, with different expectations of men and women. It is considered all right for an older man to become involved with a younger woman, for instance, but the reverse is seldom acceptable. Women portrayed as desirable in the mass media are young and beautiful, and since Americans have made a fetish of the young female body, a myriad of products is available to help women deny physical aging. Femininity is equated with reproductive abilities or sex appeal. Attractive or desirable men, on the other hand, are presented as potent, and potency is equated with power and control. Generally, men continue to increase in power (socially, if not physically) at least through middle age, while women lose their "femininity" and value as they age.

In old age women who have built identities as wives and mothers are statistically unlikely to be either. We live in a mobile society, and children are likely to live far away from parents. Most women sixty-five or older are alone, widowed, or divorced, and more than a third of them live below the federal poverty level. Elderly women have even fewer role models than middle-aged or younger women and also have fewer of the things that help us through life —money, health, friends, and work. Many women end their lives in nursing homes or hospitals, once again totally dependent on others, but this time alone.

By coming together, organizing themselves, and counseling each other, women are beginning to improve these situations and are making themselves heard—loud and clear—on the job, in the media, and in the courts. Consciousness-raising groups, support groups (e.g., mothers' groups, divorce and separation groups, and career counseling groups), and simple discussions between friends are typical forums for creatively resolving what seem to be insurmountable problems. Therapy, too, can be a process through which to explore feelings and needs and perhaps learn how to do something about them. But therapy has a limited usefulness if it fails to take into account the fact that personal problems women experience often grow out of the social roles we are expected to fill.

Psychotherapy for Women

Making the decision to enter therapy isn't a pleasant task or one that most people feel happy about (except perhaps those who view it from the start as an exercise in personal growth). You may experience relief when you have finally contacted a therapist; but the thought of confiding in a stranger, dredging up painful memories, or looking at yourself in a critical way is nobody's idea of a good time.

However, that doesn't mean that it cannot be a beneficial and rewarding experience. If there is a possibility that you might see a therapist (and there has been for one out of every ten people in this country), you must set about educating yourself in order to know what to expect and what to look for, and to know your options and your rights. By reading this book and perhaps talking to women who have been, or are currently in, therapy you can help yourself to have the kind of therapy experience you will be happy with.

As a result of consumer pressure, more therapists are now aware that women want and deserve therapy that takes into account the specific life experience of women, and they have begun to pay more attention to women's needs. Many are changing their traditional attitudes toward the psychology of women and are taking into consideration the impact of women's changing social role. Some therapists now actually specialize in women's issues.

The impact of the rising tide of consumerism on psychotherapy has been significant, and the Women's Movement has played an increasingly large role in the way women are treated. It has given women the words to express how they have been dissatisfied and what they want—to assume responsibility for, and control over, their own lives. Women consumers have forced the psychotherapy profession to take a hard look at what it has done quite routinely —reinforce sex role stereotypes—and to make changes.

The therapists who are paying attention to their women clients will obviously be the ones chosen when there are alternatives. Unfortunately, in some parts of the country the number of therapists available may be limited. But, even in such a situation, it is important that you choose as wisely as possible. Because women clients are now making known what they want—therapists who are aware of, and respect, their special needs—they are having a profound effect on the way therapy is practiced in this country.

Chapter

2

The Double
Standard of
Mental Health

The first thing that any woman considering therapy should recognize is that most traditional forms of therapy operate on assumptions that are basically destructive to women (although some techniques, as we will show, may be adequately modified to be helpful). Many therapists do not question the validity of sex-role stereotypes. It is important to understand how the stereotype implies that a woman not only *is* a certain way, she is *supposed* to be that way, and in all probability will *always* be that way. It is also important to look at how the traditional therapist views the woman who does not conform to the stereotype, and the resulting implications for her.

Most people, including many therapists, believe in the myth that therapy is "value free," meaning that the therapist is totally objective and does not impose any personal beliefs or opinions on the therapy process. Therapists, like anyone else, however, are affected by cultural values, and definitions of mental health reflect the stereotypes.

The Stereotypes

A woman is submissive, passive, narcissistic, and dependent. Her goal in life is to marry, have children, and be loved. She is the emotional support for men and children. She is selfless, thinking first of others, and putting herself last. She lives vicariously through others. She is incapable of thinking abstractly and personalizes the world. Her self-esteem is shaped by what others think of her; she is appearance-oriented. She is other-directed. Her moods are controlled by her hormones. She is emotional, irrational, easily distracted, fickle, artistic, and silly.

A man is aggressive, active, objective, and independent. His goal in life is to achieve, to be somebody, and to leave his mark on the world. He gets his emotional support from a woman. He puts his career first and takes his family for granted; he is competitive. He lives for himself. He thinks in abstractions and deals with the world impersonally. His self-esteem is derived from his accomplishments; he is performance-oriented. He is inner-directed. His moods do not fluctuate. He is unemotional, rational, stable, dependable, scientific, dominant, and serious.

The Broverman Study

These stereotypes are clearly evidenced in a series of studies published by Inge Broverman and her colleagues in 1970. They designed tests so that the clinicians involved would have to choose between two descriptions; for example, "not at all aggressive" or "very aggressive," "very home oriented" or "very worldly," "very talkative" or "not at all talkative," "unable to separate feelings from ideas" or "easily separates feelings from ideas," "easily expresses tender feelings" or "does not express tender feelings at all." The seventy-nine clinicians (thirty-three women and forty-six men) were then divided into three groups. One group was told to "think of normal adult men and then indicate for each pair which item best described a mature, healthy, socially competent adult *man.*" The next group was told to indicate the items that most accurately described a "mature, healthy, socially competent adult *woman.*" The third group was to check the descriptions which more accurately described a "healthy, mature, socially competent adult *person.*"

When the results were tabulated, there were very few differences between the descriptions of the normal, healthy, adult man and the descriptions of the normal, healthy, adult person. However, the description of the normal, healthy adult woman was exactly the opposite of both. In the views of the clinicians, she differed from both the healthy man and the healthy person by being "more submissive, less independent, less adventurous, more easily influenced, less aggressive, less competitive, more excitable in minor crises, having her feelings more easily hurt, more conceited about her appearance, less objective, and disliking math and science." In other words, a healthy woman is an unhealthy adult; for a woman to be a healthy adult, she must act masculine. It was also noted that both the male and female clinicians held this view.

The study highlights the double bind for women who are in therapy:

There are two standards of mental health—one for adult males and adult people, another for adult women. Should a woman change toward being a healthy adult, she becomes sick as a woman.

As a matter of fact, the clinical definition of hysteria is remarkably close to the clinical definition of femininity. Even the word *hysteria* comes from the Greek word for uterus; for some time hysterial illness was thought to be caused by a wandering uterus which had come to rest at the affected part of the body. To this day hysterectomies (removal of the uterus) are often performed on women to control depression, irritability, and mood swings.

We feel that many therapists are of the opinion (usually not openly acknowledged or expressed) that if women are supposed to be passive, if their goal is to marry and have children, then a woman who is active, unmarried, and childless is abnormal, strange, confusing, and ought to be unhappy. If a woman is passive, married, and a mother, then she is normal, easy to understand, and ought to be happy. Many therapists suggest that the woman who deviates from her feminine role is potentially destructive to herself and her family. For example, a woman who does not fit the stereotype of the "good mother" will probably be held responsible for any mental disturbance in her child. Many marriage problems may be considered the fault of a woman who is too independent or earns more money than her husband. Situations continue to exist in which a therapist will accept for treatment a woman sent by her husband because she is "letting herself go" and not making herself attractive to him.

Women who entrust themselves to therapists with attitudes such as these are likely to get worse rather than better. The basically negative attitude of the therapist will confirm and add to the woman's feelings of inadequacy. Moreover, the therapist's definition of a healthy adult female encourages a return to the very behavior which necessitated treatment in the first place.

The potential dangers for women in therapy are twofold: first, they may be treated by a therapist who practices a type of therapy whose very foundations and tenets are based on the idea that women are basically inferior mirror images of men; second, they may be treated by someone who practices a therapy that in theory is neutral and nonjudgmental, but the therapist her/himself may still have the biases shown by the Broverman study.

A New Standard for Therapy

What can help women is therapy where the rigid role expectations are relaxed and people are free to choose their lives; where what is good for *human persons* is the focus; where the androgynous person is the goal. It is done in a manner that builds the person's strengths. The therapist is not the god; there are two equals.

If it is true (and we believe it is) that your therapist's values will influence the outcome of therapy, then it becomes crucial that you have a clear sense of what those values are. Women are now interviewing therapists and asking questions like "how do you feel about working mothers?" And therapists who reject the double standard of mental health are able to answer these questions satisfactorily because they are aware of their own values.

The kind of therapist you should look for is one who has thought through her/his attitudes toward women and examined her/his therapeutic methods for sexist or discriminatory biases. Your therapist should be nonsexist, meaning that s/he assumes you will make decisions about your behavior based on what you want for and from yourself and not on what is expected of you because of your sex. S/he should be informed about the struggles of women in our society and incorporate this perspective into her/his day-to-day contact with women clients.

You can expect that your therapist will not use the power of her/his position to reinforce "appropriate" feminine behavior or punish "inappropriate" masculine behavior. You may think of your therapist as a role model or as an expert in human relationships; but be aware that s/he probably has not solved all her own problems, nor will s/he be able to solve all of yours.

Finally, an important part of therapy for women is education in how to make contact with other women who may be able to offer support. The most common problem women clients deal with is isolation, and a major thrust of effective therapy should be to overcome this. A good therapist doesn't push her/his client to join any particular organization, but s/he can provide information on groups offering consciousness-raising, health services, or women's cultural events. This educational function, although not a primary focus of therapy, can serve as a bridge between the work you do in your therapist's office and the changes you make in your daily life.

Characteristics of a Good Psychotherapist

Women who have found therapy helpful consistently report certain personality characteristics in their therapists: *empathy,* or the ability to understand another's feelings; *warmth,* or showing care and concern for others; and *genuineness,* or the ability to be open and direct. No matter what the theoretical approach of the therapist, effective therapists are *attentive, natural, willing to give direct reassurance, are not overly critical,* and *are willing to share some of their feelings with clients.* Therapists who are not helpful are detached, aloof, passive, neutral, use abstract language, cause the client to experience anger, and make her feel like "just another client." A young woman who is currently in therapy feels that "what makes a therapist effective is caring about the client, honesty, sensitivity to timing, skill, allowing the client to lead, and the courage to try new things."

Besides the personality characteristics of your therapist and the philosophical or psychological theory to which s/he subscribes, you will want to know about her/his particular background and training. Psychotherapy crosses many professional lines and its practitioners are drawn from the ranks of counselors, social workers, doctors, nurses, psychologists, analysts and many others. Different disciplines have different ranges of treatment available to them. For example, it is a rare psychiatrist who does not prescribe drugs (although not necessarily to all patients), while most psychologists or psychiatric social workers, for instance, use drugs only when they have an ongoing relationship with a medical practitioner, such as in a clinic or institution. Basically, you need to be aware of whether your therapist's training is medical or non-medical.

The fact is that research has consistently failed to find any correlation between methods, techniques, or even results and a therapist's espoused school or system. Therapists do differ from one another, but their professional training, their credentials or lack of credentials, and the theoretical positions they adhere to are poor indicators of the real differences. When you are looking for a therapist, keep in mind that the therapist's credentials are less important than her/his personality and values. Your therapist's personality is a critical factor in determining the outcome of your therapy experience.

Many of the skills that therapists learn seem to be things which everyone can learn—listening, understanding what motivates people, an ability to hear what a person is saying underneath the surface, or picking up patterns in a person's life. However, a good therapist has the resources to handle needs that may be too great for your friends or family to handle. A therapist is a professional in the area of psychology, but s/he is not a magician. What you can get out of therapy depends basically on you—on how willing you are to take a good look at the way you live your life and how ready you are to make changes if you are dissatisfied with what you find.

What Can You Expect?

If you have had no experience with therapy, you will probably have trouble imagining what it is like or what you can expect of it. Each individual is different, so there is no way to tell you what therapy will be like for you. Therefore, we decided simply to quote here how other women have felt about going into therapy.

My preconceptions came mostly from the media, i.e. couches, male therapists with beards, drugs, shock therapy, white strait-jackets, and very expensive private doctors.

I thought that therapists would pick small behavioristic tendencies and try to interpret them with the wordy complexities from some textbook. I thought that they would look for aberrations in the most innocent and simple behaviors.

I thought that therapists were "magicians"—knew the right answers—and if I just did what I was "supposed" to, my life would be better. I now know that the process of therapy is difficult work demanding honesty with yourself as well as with the therapist.

I thought that the therapist could/would tell me what to do and I would/could do it and everything would be fine. I thought that just by talking things out and knowing why I felt a certain way, it would automatically change. I thought you could force yourself to change. None of that is true for me.

I walked in wanting my therapist to tell me what to do with my life and make "it" all better. My experience has helped me understand that I am responsible for making "it" better as well as taking care of myself, making decisions, etc.

My therapist taught me to question—for perhaps the first time—how *I* feel about things. She helped me realize that I'm not responsible for other people's (my husband's) feelings and that I don't need to feel guilty if he chooses not to be happy. I also know that I'm not alone in my feelings.

The major incorrect preconception I had about therapy was that the therapist would help me solve all of my problems, and after she identified all of these problems I would be on the road to getting my life together in three easy sessions. But I soon realized it doesn't work like that. The therapist helps and supports you in this process, but it still all basically comes from you.

I had very old attitudes which said go to a therapist when you're in crisis and need help. I never saw therapy as an ongoing process for me to grow and change. This has occurred through my experience in seeing myself change old patterns of being.

Originally I joined some weekend groups mostly out of curiosity. Later I became aware that I needed help sorting out some scary and confusing feelings. Now I view therapy as a means to help growing and becoming more clear, alive and solidly myself. Therapy has highlighted some important issues for me, such as reclaiming my power, being more assertive and emphasizing the importance of feeling capable and self-sufficient.

Chapter
3
Psychotherapy for Women

In order to discuss how therapy has changed to meet the needs of women, it is necessary to first describe how women themselves have changed. The Women's Movement, perhaps the most significant bloodless revolution in history, has touched the lives of all of us in so many areas —education, industry, art and music, government and politics, law and domestic relations, as well as psychology.

The 1960s and 1970s saw a rise in social and political activism across the United States, primarily focusing on civil rights and anti-Vietnam War activity. Many women who involved themselves in these struggles to end the oppression of other people, found that they were developing an awareness of their own oppression. Women active in Students for a Democratic Society (SDS), in anti-war groups, and in many grass-roots organizing projects found themselves once again relegated to the typewriter and the coffeepot. Even women representing large organizations, such as Women Strike for Peace or the Women's International League for Peace and Freedom, found that in rallies or coalition meetings of many groups they were seen as token women and were often competing with each other for the one spot available to women's groups.

Having gained new skills from their political experiences, women began working together to meet their own needs. All across the country, women's organizations sprang to life, from local consciousness-raising groups made up of neighborhood friends, to large efforts dealing with major issues such as health care and abortion, to national organizations such as the National Organization for Women (NOW) and the Women's Political Caucus. Many of these groups came up with similar ideas at the same time, the results of hundreds of women thinking and acting together, even though often separated by distance, political affiliation, and education.

Some women found strength and a new awareness of themselves in the sense of sisterhood they gained in the Women's Movement. They also took pride in reclaiming the history of the earlier feminist movement of the late 1800s and early 1900s. For many women it was a new awakening of pride, an awakening which changed their lives irreversibly.

The majority of women had no direct contact with the Women's Movement (and denied that they were "women's libbers") but were still touched by the waves of energy sent out by others. They began to question discrimination on the job, lack of services such as child care and health care in their communities, and sexist attitudes on the part of employers, educators, or doctors.

Demand for Better Therapy

Old problems of alienation, loneliness, or lack of self-esteem did not necessarily disappear with the advent of the Women's Movement. These problems still existed and had to be dealt with in new ways. Women formed support groups, living collectives, work groups, women's centers

and consciousness-raising groups to help spread information and provide support for all women. But many women
still felt the need for the option of individual or group
psychotherapy. The Women's Movement had provided a
heightened awareness of the sexism and oppression of
women which have often been a part of traditional therapy, so women began seeking a new kind of psychotherapy
which would provide help but not ask them to surrender
their political beliefs or their burgeoning sense of self.

This woman's story is typical of the influence of the
Women's Movement on personal therapy.

I first entered therapy eleven years ago for nine months. I didn't
know about any Women's Movement, so a lot of what I did in
terms of my own growth and autonomy was based on what my
own intuition said was right for me, even though I knew of no
role models at the time and was isolated. As I have been exposed
to and become part of the Women's Movement, it has given me
a lot of affirmation; it has helped me to break up isolation and has
helped me give language to thoughts and feelings I have previously had difficulty articulating.

Other women tell stories of confusing or unhappy relationships with former therapists. One said of her therapy
with a psychologist:

I was confused by my therapist. He seemed straightforward and
not uncomfortable with who I was, but then I noticed that he
complimented me every time I wore a skirt and told me I "looked
good." I thought I looked good even in my jeans, and I had been
fighting for years having to "dress properly." When I asked him
about this, he said he was trying to help my sense of self-esteem.
He said that of course I didn't have to wear dresses and all that
other stuff, but didn't I want to look attractive? Does this mean
I have to look attractive to him?

Women began to seek help through women's centers or
from therapists who identified themselves as interested in
women's problems. These women were not always femi-

nists; they just wanted someone whom they felt they could trust to support the beginnings of their independence and not feed their insecurities and dependence. Often women in this position did not know where to turn. If they did not have strong ties to the women's community in their area, or if there was no women's community near them, they had trouble finding a dependable referral source who could recommend a competent therapist.

Women Psychotherapists

A parallel movement in the development of a psychotherapy for women was taking place among women therapists who became involved in the Women's Movement. Women who were already therapists began to look with their own new women's consciousness at the sexist values they had been taught in school and were using in their practices. Many decided they wanted to create a new therapy for women which would value women as independent, creative, and first-class people, rather than devalue them as dependent, hysterical, or inferior to men. These therapists were attempting to create new attitudes in therapy rather than just new and different techniques. They modified various therapeutic techniques in order to eliminate sexist values and retain aspects positive to women.

Gay Rights

Until recently, homosexuality was defined by the psychiatric establishment as a disease. Even though the diagnosis of *homosexuality* has recently been dropped by the American Psychiatric Association, lesbians still find that, for the most part, their experience in therapy usually involves being challenged about their sexual preference and having the real and serious problems for which they are seeking help pushed aside. Many therapists continue to insist that the "real" issue is the client's sexuality, and any attempt to discuss other issues is termed "denial." Lesbians have been hospitalized, drugged, even subjected to psychosurgery, in attempts to "cure" them of their so-called deviant sexuality.

The development of a women's therapy has been shaped to some extent by the need to abolish discrimination against lesbians. The fact of a woman's lesbianism is still used by some therapists as a weapon to deny her custody of children, an excuse for incarceration in a mental hospital, and an automatic classification of her as unable to perform day-to-day tasks of living. A number of groups, such as the Boston NOW Lesbian Task Force, have made it a priority to articulate the problems lesbians face and to find therapists who are lesbians themselves or who will deal with lesbians as they would with any woman.

Research on the Psychology of Women

Until very recently, almost no literature had been written on the psychology of women. Within the last ten years, however, there has been a veritable explosion of research by women in the fields of psychology, sociology, and health care. This research has revealed that the experience of being female in our society is the basis for many of the emotional problems that trouble women and may eventually bring them to therapy. A review of some of the current literature on the developmental stages of girls through childhood and adolescence reveals many potential problems. Cultural expectations of femininity are first conveyed to daughters by their mothers in many ways far more subtle than by dressing them in pink clothing, and giving them dolls and hair ribbons. Girls in our society are expected to be less assertive (docile and "ladylike"), be more dependent (sensitive and intuitive), to avoid rough-housing or fighting, to have greater self-control (earlier and easier toilet-training) and to have stronger sexual inhibitions than boys. Since children are cared for almost exclusively by their mothers or other women, girls learn through identification that they are expected to care for others. The result is that a girl develops less of a sense of herself and more of a sense of depending on other people than is expected of a boy.

Because, as has been recently discovered, girls are physiologically and neurologically better coordinated than boys, infant girls are more responsive to being physically soothed and talked to by their mothers. Studies show that girl babies are held more and are more sensitive to things they hear than are boy babies. This seems to automatically involve them in a closer, more passive relationship with their mothers.

Little girls are encouraged to socialize and chatter with their mothers rather than be out doing things. Most mothers worry more about the physical safety of daughters, and the worry and hesitation in the mother's face make the little girl cautious, thus making it hard for her to let go with daring and abandonment during the toddler period. She learns to believe that she is more fragile than a boy, so she becomes more docile and stays closer to her mother. She never quite gains a sense of her body's capabilities or of active mastery of the world. Instead of developing a spontaneous self-confidence in her own body, the little girl shows hesitation in her exploration of the world around her. Later a little girl is often ill-prepared to face the turmoil of separation from mother, and she may have a poorly-defined identity as a separate person.

In grade school girls are far more likely than boys to withdraw from threatening situations or to seek help from adults and peers because they have not been encouraged to be independent, but on the contrary have always received approval for the act of seeking help and cooperating with teachers. It is this need for approval rather than for achievement that motivates girls to perform well during grade school and high school, when academic success is not only accepted, but expected of them. However, by fifth grade girls already show a tendency toward avoiding success. Grace Baruch, in a study through the National Institute of Child Health and Human Development, asked a group of fifth-grade girls to write a story beginning, "Ann has won first prize in the science fair for her exhibit on car engines." More than half the girls wrote that Ann had lost friends, shared the prize with others, become unhappy with the prize, or—unbelievably—that the judges had later realized they had made a mistake!

Adolescent girls are inundated with advice from parents, peers, and magazine articles on how to attract boys. Much of that advice has a negative effect on a girl's self-esteem, since she is usually exhorted to be beautiful, slim, and acne-free, to lose at the games she plays with boys, and to develop an interest in the boy's interest, often at the expense of her own.

When a girl begins menstruating, it becomes her responsibility to say "yes" or "no" to sex with boys. Whether a girl is a "nice girl" or "cheap" depends on her ability to control her sexuality. Herein lie the roots of many women's sexual inhibitions, their reluctance to show pleasure by participating actively in sex. If, deep down, one believes that sex is dirty or wrong for a "nice girl," then being open and frankly sexual becomes difficult if not impossible.

Teenage girls often develop sexual feelings about other girls or older women. These feelings are more difficult to cope with than those toward boys, which are at least acknowledged as common. Most girls never realize that other girls and women have experienced similar feelings. In recent years a slightly more permissive attitude has developed toward adult women who openly admit their lesbianism; but the idea that teenagers are often coping with similar emotions is rarely acknowledged.

A study conducted at the University of California at Berkeley shows that men increase their sense of personal confidence consistently during the years from junior high through their thirties. In contrast, women in their thirties

were less sure of themselves than they had been as teenagers. The growing body of literature on the psychology
of women indicates that *from birth* women are put in
the double-bind of being encouraged to achieve at school
or at work, but not to the extent of losing their "femininity."

Part
II

Schools
of Therapy

When you start looking for a therapist, you will find your-
self faced with a bewildering array of types of therapy
and approaches to problem solving from which to choose.
Some therapists identify themselves with a particular
theoretical school, indicating that they have studied that
philosophical approach and apply it in their therapy;
others simply use techniques grouped under a particular
name. There are far too many different schools of psycho-
logical theory for us to cover here, but we will discuss
those which have been dominant in the United States and
are relevant to the majority of today's clinicians.

We will also be looking at the ways in which various
schools of therapy actually treat women. Theoretical for-
mulations may sound neutral, but their practice in re-
gard to women often leaves much to be desired. We call
attention to groups who have left out specific reference to
women or the needs of women, because to do so is to ne-
glect the fact of sexist discrimination against women not

*only by society at large but by the psychiatric and psycho-
logical establishment.*

*Most of these therapies may be conducted individually,
with couples, or in groups. There are many different kinds
of groups, and you should expect that a group leader will
be able to tell you in your interview something about the
group, the way it will be run, and what will be expected
of you as a group member. Some leaders take a laissez-
faire attitude, sitting back and allowing group members
to interact in any way they want; others have a very tight
structure, do a lot of intervening, and exert a strong influence on the group. You can expect the leader to take responsibility for the group but not to do all the work of the
group. Group members should not be permitted to attack
one another, and the group leader should not attack or
humiliate anyone. Also, statements made within a group
are confidential; neither you nor anyone else should discuss group business with outsiders.*

*The descriptions we give in this book will give you an
idea of what each school of therapy is like. If a particular
approach appeals to you (or is highly recommended to
you), check the suggested readings and do some follow-up
to find out more about it. The following are questions you
might ask about any approach to therapy:*

• Does it focus on growth in general or concentrate on
particular symptoms?

• Does it emphasize control of the process by the therapist or cooperative efforts by the therapist and client?

• Does it look at internal (intrapsychic, psychodynamic)
problems or emphasize external relationships with the
environment?

• Does it investigate the roots of the problem in the past
or does it work on issues of current functioning?

• Is the goal of therapy an intellectual understanding of

past experience or the integration of feelings, body and thought?

• Is there a developmental theory which states that women are biologically inferior to men? Does it use biological differences as an excuse for keeping women in an inferior position?

The answers to these questions can give you a starting place in deciding on the right therapist for you, but it cannot be the final determinant. The most important issue in a therapy relationship—and one to which we will return again and again—is how you feel about the therapist. You need to know how the therapist views people, how much awareness s/he has of the external oppression facing women as well as the psychological problems which need to be dealt with, and how much s/he has reflected on her/his role in the therapy process. After all, the two of you are engaged in a mutual process for your benefit, and only you can decide if that other person can be helpful.

Chapter 4

The Talking Cure

Freudian Psychoanalysis

ORIGINS

Sigmund Freud was born in 1856 and lived most of his life in Vienna, Austria. He left Austria for England (where he died in 1939) only when the Nazi Occupation drove him out. Freud was the oldest of eight children born of his father's second marriage. He was graduated from the University of Vienna Medical School in 1881, and planned an academic and research career. The combination of the needs of his family and children and the fact that chances of academic advancement were limited for a Jew led him to begin a private practice in psychiatry. In 1885 Freud studied hypnotism with Jean Charcot, a French psychiatrist noted for his work with hypnosis. Attempting to use hypnosis with his patients, Freud became disenchanted with it when he felt the results he obtained were only temporary, and neurotic symptoms alleviated through hypnotism reappeared in other forms. Then, through collaboration with Joseph Breuer and the use of Breuer's technique of "talking out" or "free association," Freud began to develop a new concept of the unconscious. In 1895 Freud and Breuer collaborated on a book about hysteria, but they soon parted ways as Freud continued developing his theory that the origins of neurosis were to be found in unconscious sexual conflicts.

In 1900 Freud published the first of his major works, *The Interpretation of Dreams,* followed by *Three Contributions to the Sexual Theory.* His theory of infantile sexuality brought him into conflict with many of his colleagues but also marked the beginning of his position as the founder of psychoanalysis. A group of disciples, including Alfred Adler and Carl Jung, and sometimes referred to as the Vienna Circle, formed around him. Together they formed the First Congress of Psychoanalysis and, later, the International Psychoanalytical Association. Jung and Adler split with Freud within a few years to form their own schools of therapy.

Freud remained in Vienna until 1938 when he was persuaded to leave for London because of the danger posed to him and his family by the Nazis. Although plagued for the last sixteen years of his life by recurring cancer of the mouth and jaw, Freud continued to see patients and perform self-analysis until his death in 1939.

BASIC THEORY

Psychoanalytic theory operates on the premise that most mental processes occur on an unconscious level, and that nervous disorders have their roots in unconscious sexual conflicts. Freud saw both adults and children as motivated primarily by instinctual drives, chief among them the libido, or sexual energy. Personality is organized gradually into three parts: the *id,* or instinctual drives which are seeking expression; the *superego,* or internalized parental restrictions and demands; and the *ego,* the self which mediates between the demands of the id and the restrictions of the superego. As the child goes through the stages of libidinal development (called oral, anal, and phallic), each stage must be resolved so that he or she can pass to the next. Unconscious conflicts which remain unresolved will later in life produce neurotic symptoms (behavior which helps to ward off anxiety, but which may cause problems of its own, such as phobias or compulsions).

Freud's psychoanalytic theories permanently altered both the treatment of mental illness and the conceptualization of human personality growth and development. With the exception of Behavior Modification, most forms of therapy in this country owe their origins to Freud, either directly or because the progenitors of new therapies were originally trained as Freudians. Many changes in the original theory, and especially in the original mode of practice, have taken place over the years, and many therapies have explicitly denied or broken with certain aspects of Freudian theory; but the debt remains. Most theorists do not dispute the existence of the unconscious, the importance of childhood experience, or the significance of sexuality; but they wrangle endlessly over the specific interpretations of these phenomena. In fact, many of Freud's most faithful followers, such as Jung, broke with him over his continued emphasis on sexuality and sexual conflicts as causes of nervous problems.

TREATMENT

Freud, in lecturing to new students, described the process of psychoanalysis as lacking the drama attendant on some other forms of medical treatment: "In psychoanalytic treatment nothing happens but an exchange of words between the patient and the physician. The patient talks, tells of his past experiences and present impressions, complains, and expresses his wishes and his emotions. The physician listens, attempts to direct the patient's thought-processes, reminds him, forces his attention in certain directions, gives him explanations and observes the reactions of understanding or denial thus evoked."[1]

In classical psychoanalytic therapy, the patient meets with the analyst three to five times a week for forty-five or fifty minutes per session. After a brief introductory period of talking face-to-face, the patient lies on a couch with the analyst seated out of sight behind the couch. The patient is encouraged to learn the process of free association and say anything which comes to mind, no matter how trivial. The analyst usually limits her/his statements to interpretations of the material presented. Lying on the couch is meant to encourage the flow of unconscious material from the patient, and the analyst's remaining quiet and out of sight provides the minimum of interference with the patient's feelings.

The analytic process may take from two to five years (or more). Some analysts, especially more traditional ones, ask patients not to talk about their analysis or read any psychological material while in analysis. They may also require that patients agree to make no major life changes during the analysis (such as marriage, divorce, or job changes).

They (little girls) notice the penis of a brother or playmate, strikingly visible and of large proportions, at once recognize it as the superior counterpart of their own small and inconspicuous organ, and from that time forward fall victim to envy of the penis. . . . After a woman has become aware of the wound of her narcissism, she develops, like a scar, a sense of inferiority. When she has passed beyond her first attempt at explaining her lack of a penis as being a punishment personal to herself and has realized that sexual character is a universal one, she begins to share the contempt felt by men for a sex which is the lesser in so important a respect.

Freud, *Some Psychological Consequences of the Anatomical Distinctions between the Sexes,* 1925

EVALUATION OF THEORY

Evaluation of Freudian theory is difficult because it covers a vast range of ideas and practice. Freud himself wrote many volumes, and ideas developed in his early writings were often modified in his later ones. His followers have been no less prolific, and each year hundreds of journal articles and dozens of books are published dealing with every aspect of Freudian psychotherapy. Because of the impossibility of evaluating all of this adequately, we are limiting our comments to areas which have been widely criticized by women in psychology.

One such area is Freud's developmental theory. He postulates that a girl discovers early in life that her sexual organs are not only different from, but inferior to, the penis of a boy, and that she develops an envy of the "superior" male equipment, which shapes her whole growth and development. From this formulation of penis envy came Freud's conclusions about successful maturation for women. Girls must sublimate their desire for a penis by growing up to marry and have a baby, which represents the longed-for penis. If the baby is male, it allows complete gratification of the sublimated wish.

From this theory of psychological development there follows a number of concepts about what makes a "good" or "feminine" woman, such as passivity and acceptance of a so-called biologically-determined role as nurturer of children and of men. Women who insist on the possibility of other roles for themselves are defined as neurotic and in need of treatment.

We strongly disagree with this theory about the formation of a woman's personality and the consequences for her role in life. Freud's statements about penis envy were not based on objective observation, but purely on his personal belief in the superiority of the male and the male organ and in the moral correctness of that belief. Later theorists have suggested that women may legitimately envy the position and power of men in society, but not the possession of a penis.

Another area of Freud's theories with which we take issue is his statement that there are two kinds of orgasm, vaginal and clitoral. According to Freud, women who perceive their orgasms as originating in the clitoris or from any activity other than heterosexual intercourse, are immature, frigid, or fixated at an infantile level of sexual development. He postulated that a mature, feminine woman should obtain sexual satisfaction from orgasm originating in the vagina and occurring during intercourse, recognizing her true biological relationship to a man as the instrument of sexual satisfaction. Since recent studies[2] show that all female orgasms originate in the clitoris, no matter how they are perceived, and that all orgasms are similar, no matter what kind of activity stimulates them, women who are confronted with traditional Freudian beliefs are in a difficult position: they must deny the evidence of these studies, deny their own experience, or deny their analyst.

At first glance these issues may seem far removed from the problems which bring you to therapy and from issues you plan to discuss with your therapist; but they have the effect of skewing the way a therapist views a patient and the underlying motives which will be ascribed to a patient, whether they are openly discussed or not. Many therapists have preconceived ideas of women's proper role, based on their own definitions of femininity. This has particularly serious consequences for lesbians, since Freudian theory views homosexuality as a perversion.

With the development of puberty, the maturing of the female sexual organs, which up till then have been in a condition of latency, seems to bring about an intensification of the original narcissism, and this is unfavourable to the development of a true object-love with its accompanying sexual over-estimation; there arises in the woman a certain self-sufficiency (especially when there is a ripening into beauty) which compensates her for the social restrictions upon her object-choice. Strictly speaking, such women love only themselves with an intensity comparable to that of the man's love for them. Nor does their need lie in the direction of loving, but of being loved; and that man finds favour with them who fulfills this condition.

Freud, *On Narcissism,* 1914

EVALUATION OF TREATMENT

There are a number of other issues which must also be considered and evaluated by any woman contemplating psychoanalytic treatment. Psychoanalysis requires a considerable investment of time and money. Treatment generally consists of three to four sessions weekly, and each session can cost from $40 to $60. Even at minimal rates (which may be obtained by consulting an analyst in training at a psychoanalytic institute in many of the large cities), the cost may amount to several thousand dollars per year. As a result, women who undertake analysis tend to be in the upper or upper-middle economic classes. These women may have flexible work schedules and probably consider such a financial commitment to therapy a priority. Since analysts tend to come from similar class backgrounds, most of the information being fed back into the analytic system will reflect only the needs, attitudes, and concerns of those classes, and it therefore remains a closed system.

Another problem built into, and encouraged by, psychoanalysis is the mystification of the therapy process. An analyst will usually refuse to answer questions about her/ himself (to heighten the transference or the strong positive and negative feelings toward the analyst) and discourage discussion about the analysis or any reading about the psychotherapeutic process (to minimize resistance or the tendency of the patient to fight the process). In this way the analyst bolsters an already strong societal view of her/ himself as the expert with a special knowledge that is unavailable to ordinary people. Because the analyst is often male and the patient usually female, the stereotype of a knowledgeable, strong man helping a weak, dependent woman may therefore be reinforced. Patients have difficulty in effectively challenging this mystification, because any criticism of the analyst and any questioning of the analytic method is interpreted by the analyst as resistance to being "cured," no matter how legitimate the patient's criticism may be.

Another problem that has recently come to light is that this particular treatment process tends to make patients sexually vulnerable to analysts. The analytic process involves transference—strong feelings on the part of the patient for and about the analyst which have been "transferred" from other people in the patient's past. The transference feelings may be negative or positive, and many analysts expect that patients will fall in love with the doctor. Correctly handled, these feelings can be a key to the resolution of a woman's problems; but the psychoanalytic profession has ignored the evidence that many analysts have difficulty in dealing appropriately with the strong transference feelings of their women patients. Women have complained that they have been told by analysts that sexual intercourse with the analyst would benefit them by making them more loving and that, since the intercourse was part of their treatment, they were still expected to pay the analyst. Other women, attempting to complain about such treatment, or to lodge complaints with other analysts, have been told that they were being seductive and simply fantasizing that a sexual relationship had occurred because they desired it. Only recently was an analyst successfully prosecuted by a patient who claimed that he had sexual relations with her as part of "treatment." In her book, *Betrayal,*[3] Julie Roy shows that the dependence of a confused and upset woman on an analyst leaves her open and vulnerable to the abuse of trust. Sexual abuse is by no means limited to analysts, but the structure of that particular relationship and the encouragement of strong transference and dependence creates an atmosphere in which positive transference may be confused with genuine mutual attraction.

Neo-Freudians or the Cultural School

ORIGINS

From 1900 onwards, Freud's ideas stirred great debate. He was subjected to many harsh criticisms and received equally passionate support from his followers. As more debate and exploration took place, students and colleagues whom Freud regarded as close followers began to separate themselves from him, many later forming new psychoanalytic societies and institutes for the study of their own theories of psychoanalysis. Students split with Freud for many reasons: personality conflicts with Freud (who did not tolerate differences well); differences of opinion about theoretical emphasis; and the perceived need to pursue new lines of thought. We have grouped together under the title of Neo-Freudians or the Cultural School some of the best-known Freudians who remained fairly close to traditional theory but definitely separated themselves from Freud. This separation took place over many years, much of it a gradual process as the analysts grew more experienced and developed their own ideas in depth.

The chief point of disagreement with Freudian theory for the Neo-Freudians has been the rejection of the libido theory or regarding the sexual drives as the root of all problems and the most important determinant in the formation of the personality. Instead, the Neo-Freudians have moved toward a more cultural or social interpretation of problems in people's lives. The focus has shifted from a preoccupation with sexuality to closer examination of interpersonal relations (sometimes referred to as *object relations*). Most Neo-Freudians still emphasize important aspects of Freudian theory: the idea that early childhood experience is important, that neurosis has its roots in the developmental process, and that infantile sexuality does exist. Most still use analysis as the major means of treatment for mental problems, but many have modified the language of analysis and sometimes the process, moving toward less use of the couch and more face-to-face interaction.

ALFRED ADLER AND INDIVIDUAL PSYCHOLOGY

Alfred Adler was born in Vienna in 1870 and received his medical degree in 1895 from the University of Vienna. He first specialized in ophthalmology and later switched to psychiatry. He began his association with Freud and the Vienna Psychoanalytic Society in 1902, but his place within the circle became less certain as his own ideas developed. In 1911 Adler was asked to present his views to the Psychoanalytic Society and, when he did so, was asked to resign. Adler emphasized the social nature of psychological problems and the influence that both the culture in general and other specific people had on the patient. He disagreed with the Freudian emphasis on the importance of infantile sexuality. Adler established a series of child guidance clinics in European cities in which parents and teachers could receive counseling. After 1926 Adler visited the United States regularly and finally joined the staff of the Long Island College of Medicine in 1932. He died in 1937 while on tour in Scotland.

Adler stressed understanding the individual within the environment and the choices available to her. He was the first to point out that what Freud identified as penis envy in females was probably envy of the power wielded by the possessor of a penis, not of the penis itself. In Individual Psychology, therapists have given up the use of the couch and work face-to-face with patients, often in an active and directive manner. They ask questions and help the patient to understand what "mistakes" have been fostered by her particular approach to life. The patient is encouraged to develop new patterns of behavior. There is a definite proscription of the kind of transference considered a necessity by the Freudians. Instead, the therapist acts more as an advisor or teacher, offering suggestions and encouragement to the patient, but insisting that she take responsibility for her own life. The therapist encourages social responsibility and focuses not only on the patient's own individual issues but also on the necessity for being a cooperative person in society.

KAREN HORNEY AND THE CULTURAL APPROACH

Karen Horney was born in Hamburg, Germany, in 1885. She received her medical degree from the University of Berlin in 1914 and went on to study psychiatry and psychoanalysis. She came to the United States in 1932 as associate director of the Psychoanalytic Institute in Chicago and, after two years, moved to the New York Psychoanalytic Institute. In 1941 Horney and others who shared her growing dissatisfaction with orthodox Freudian analysis founded the Association for the Advancement of Psychoanalysis and their own training institute, the American Institute of Psychoanalysis. Horney remained with both until her death in 1952.

Horney had begun early in her career to depart from traditional Freudian ideas, particularly the libido theory and penis envy. Horney's theory took a more dynamic view of the development of character structure and relied less on a biological/instinctual interpretation. Discussing Freudian analysis and her departures from it in her book *New Ways in Psychoanalysis,* Horney began the development of a female psychology that was both positive and related to the actual experiences of women. She elaborated Adler's assertion that penis envy represented a desire for male privilege and status, seeing it as a reflection of the desire of women for qualities usually regarded as masculine in our culture—independence, sexual freedom, success, and strength. Penis envy is, in her analysis, a simplistic concept, in that it supposes one answer for all women and does not investigate why women suppress their desires for the so-called masculine qualities. Horney also denounced the Freudian view that women are inherently masochistic, especially as elaborated by Helene Deutsch, a devoted Freudian follower. Deutsch insisted that women really wanted to be raped and violated, and that in their mental life they wished for humiliation. Horney decried these kinds of assertions, which had long been used to justify male violence against women.

Because of these and other ideas, Horney's colleagues in the New York Psychoanalytic Institute accused her of not resolving her own castration anxiety and of herself suffering from penis envy. Her classes at the institute were shunned, and when she was forced out, she and others formed the American Institute of Psychoanalysis.

HARRY STACK SULLIVAN AND INTERPERSONAL RELATIONS

Harry Stack Sullivan was born in 1892 in New York State and received his medical training at the Chicago College of Medicine, which he was graduated from in 1917. He studied psychiatry with William Alanson White at St. Elizabeth's Hospital in Washington, D.C., and later had formal analytic training with Clara Thompson. Sullivan worked closely with the William Alanson White Foundation (with which he remained associated for the rest of his life) on ways to make psychiatry a preventive technique, not just a method for treating mental illness. Sullivan began developing his theory of interpersonal relations in the 1930s and was strongly influenced by sociologists and anthropologists. He died in 1949.

Sullivan saw people as motivated primarily by the pursuit of satisfactions (physical needs) and the pursuit of security or a sense of well-being (culturally-determined needs). These needs can be met only in interaction with others; therefore, Sullivan felt that the study of interpersonal relations was of primary importance. Personality or the person's self-concept is formed in childhood by the reactions of significant people to the child and cannot be separated from the network of interpersonal relations. If reacted to with love, respect, and approval, the child will grow up conceiving of herself as worthy of love and esteem ("good me"). Rejection or a negative reaction to the child leads to a "bad me" concept, while disgust or anxiety on the part of others (usually parents) can lead to a "not me" concept, in which case the person is classified as extremely ill or psychotic. Sullivan believed that the personality continues to be modified through interpersonal relations throughout life.

The primary tool in Sullivanian therapy is the relationship between therapist and patient, and the therapist is recognized as an integral part of the therapy process. Interpersonal therapists have abandoned the couch for face-to-face interaction with the patient and are often directive, advising the patient on where to live, whom to spend time with, and other aspects of daily life.

CLARA THOMPSON

Clara Thompson was born in 1893 in Providence, Rhode Island. She studied at Brown University and Johns Hopkins Medical School. While studying at Johns Hopkins, she worked at St. Elizabeth's Hospital and there met William Alanson White, who influenced her later thinking. She also met, and became friends with, Harry Stack Sullivan. After completing her residency, Thompson established a private practice in Baltimore and in 1930 became the first president of the Washington-Baltimore Psychoanalytic Society. After studies abroad, Thompson moved to the

New York Institute of Psychoanalysis and became involved with Karen Horney. When Horney was forced to resign from the New York Institute, Thompson left with her. Horney went on to establish the American Institute of Psychoanalysis, while Thompson, Sullivan, and Frieda Fromm-Reichman established a New York branch of the William Alanson White Institute, where Thompson remained as executive director until her death in 1958.

Thompson made an important contribution in her series of six papers on women, written between 1941 and 1950, in which she explored the cultural experiences of women and their influence on psychological development. She did not attempt to formulate new theories of personality, recognizing that her observations were of a fairly small group and largely restricted to the upper and middle classes. Nevertheless, her observations are useful to women. Thompson was also writing about and observing women in America in the 1940s, some twenty to forty years after Freud's observations in a very different culture, and, as a consequence, dealing with different phenomena. She felt that Freud's observations may have been true for women in his time and culture, but that he ignored the effects of culture on the individual. She also pointed out that while women had gained more freedom since Freud's time they were still oppressed.

Thompson further developed ideas about a female psychology that differed from those of the traditional Freudians. She pointed out that penis envy, as described by Freud, is not the norm for all women, but rather is found in neurotic patients. She uncovered many of the conflicts and weak points in Freud's theories about women, often in a matter-of-fact way, since she had none of the fear and mistrust of women Freud seemed to have (nor did she have the need to mysticize them). When Freud criticized women for the development of rigidity and an inability to change by the age of thirty (younger than most men who show these characteristics), Thompson noted that in

Freud's time a woman of thirty literally had no future; she either had married and embarked on a career of motherhood, or had resigned herself to spinsterhood. Psychoanalysis held that there must be potential for change in order for therapy to be successful and to induce actual change in the patient's life. This potential was missing for most of the women Freud treated, and Freud himself was against women making many changes in their lives, counseling them to listen to fathers or husbands who knew what was best for them.

Thompson did not dispute Freud's observations of women (although others have), but she did argue with his interpretations of those observations. She argued, as did Horney, that Freud viewed female development solely from a male point of view, seeing the female as a negative image of the male (using the male as standard, the female as deviant), and that he saw childbearing as compensation for a missing penis, instead of seeing it as an important function in its own right, at the same time ignoring the prevalent male envy of the womb or childbearing ability in women. Her observations and criticisms were an important contribution to a new analytic viewpoint.

EVALUATION

Orthodox Freudians have many criticisms of the Neo-Freudians or Cultural School—mainly that all of these analysts have, to one degree or another, modified, changed, ignored, dropped, misinterpreted, or otherwise tampered with, the words and concepts of the master. The orthodox Freudians feel that the Cultural School has kept the form of Freudian analysis, but deviated from the correct content. They contend that the emphasis on cultural factors distorts the nature of personality development and simply delays the real analysis.

Some members of the Cultural School, particularly a branch of the Sullivanians in New York City, have been criticized for their more direct intervention in patients' lives, because it is claimed that this heightens transference feelings and leaves the way open for abuse of the therapist's power.

Criticisms have been leveled at the Neo-Freudians by the humanistic therapists as well. Many of these are the same criticisms that are directed at the orthodox Freudians: mystification of the therapy process; insistence on relinquishing power to an authority who is presumed to be guiding the patient; the use of the medical model of illness and cure; the predominance of medical training as a prerequisite for analytic training; and the lack of substantial consideration of such factors as race and class in psychoanalytical theories.

From the point of view of many women, the question of intimacy or sexual relations with the therapist arises in any of these analytic situations because of the superiority and knowledge routinely attributed to the therapist. The criticisms of the Freudians therefore also hold true in this instance. However, many Neo-Freudians have accepted less traditional views of women and may be quite flexible in their approach to treatment. If you are considering analysis, be careful to ask specific questions about the analyst's views on the basic psychology of women.

Carl Jung and Analytic Psychology

ORIGINS

Carl Jung was born in 1875 in Switzerland, the son of a Swiss Reform pastor (and the nephew of eight other pastors). He studied at the University of Basel, obtaining a medical degree in 1900, and then became interested in psychiatry. He was also interested at that time in both archeology and the occult, and several of his occult experiences led him to turn to psychiatry as a profession and as a way to search for the mysteries of the psyche. He studied in 1902 with Janet, an early teacher of Freud, and began his own investigations into the workings of the mind. He was particularly influenced by Freud's first major work, *The Interpretation of Dreams,* published in 1900.

When Jung published his first major work in 1906, a book about the significance of word association (work which he correlated with heart rate, blood pressure, and galvanic skin response—in anticipation of lie detectors), he sent Freud a copy. This initiated a correspondence and finally a meeting between the two in 1907. They exchanged visits, and Jung became the "favorite son," that is, Freud expressed the wish that he might take over leadership of the psychoanalytic movement. Their relationship was doomed to failure, however. In 1909, Freud and Jung traveled to America to lecture at Clark University in Worcester, Massachusetts, and Freud was reported to have fainted during one of their conversations, afterward accusing Jung of harboring death wishes toward him. At a later meeting in Munich in 1912, when their relationship had further cooled, Freud again fainted, foreshadowing their final break in October of 1913. Jung had assumed the presidency of the International Psychoanalytical Association in 1910, but he resigned in 1913 after the publication of "The Psychology of the Unconscious," in which he developed his theories of mythology, and in which he hypothesized that the libido was not just sexual energy, but a general psychic energy.

Jung devoted himself to private practice and the continual study of the psyche, considering psychoanalysis as one tiny part of this field. He was interested in mythology, religion, and folklore, and pursued these interests until his death in 1961. In the 1930s Jung was accused of anti-Semitism after accepting the presidency of the International General Medical Society for Psychotherapy when the Jewish psychiatrists who had filled this position and others of importance within the medical societies had resigned. He made some statements about the differences between Germanic and Jewish psychology which were easily used by the Nazis as malicious propaganda. He expressed some initial enthusiasm for the Nazi cause and later dissaffection. The charge of anti-Semitism is still leveled at Jung today, although his followers deny it.

BASIC THEORY

Jung's theories were an exploration of territory left open by Freud. Unlike the Neo-Freudians, who emphasized conscious control of behavior change, Jung explored further into the unconscious than did Freud. He proposed the idea that members of any race or culture are born with a reservoir of unconscious knowledge, myths and symbols. He called this the *collective unconscious* and felt, unlike Freud, that people were not driven by sexual instincts but rather by the myths and symbols of the race and culture into which they were born. These symbols (embodied in fairy tales, monsters, witches, heroes, the myth of the Great Mother, princesses and princes, snakes, ghosts, etc.) often appear in dreams and art, as well as manifesting themselves in neurotic symptoms. He called these symbols *archetypes,* which, he said, are by nature immutable and unchangeable, and which express qualities of the *anima* (feminine nature) and *animus* (masculine nature). Jung believed a feminine nature (feeling, maternal, and irrational) and masculine nature (logical, reasoning, and intellectual) exist in everyone. He hypothesized a neurological location for these traits but never discovered it.

Jung emphasized human spiritual needs, possibly a heritage of his religious upbringing. He strongly believed in the human need to feel a part of a universal purpose in life, which he called transcendence. Jung was the first to hypothesize that madness is not a sickness but an attempt at self-cure or a striving for a superior insight.

TREATMENT

The heart of Jungian therapy is the translation of symbolism. The therapist makes extensive use of the patient's dreams and fantasies and relates them to cultural myth and symbol. Dreams are viewed as the expression of the human need for spiritual significance and transcendence.

The goal of Jungian therapy is individuation, meaning self-discovery and the attainment of wisdom. Jung saw his therapy as particularly appropriate for people in their middle and later years, who want to experience themselves in a more complete way. Therapy provides the means to resolve the disharmony within the psyche between the conscious, the unconscious, and the collective unconscious. It is this disharmony which, Jung felt, leads to neurosis.

Jungian therapy is meant to be an experience of positive growth as well as the relief of neurotic suffering. Therapist and patient sit face-to-face and tend to have a warm and supportive relationship. There is little emphasis on transference, and the analyst maintains some detachment as s/he leads the patient into an understanding of the larger symbolic meanings of her behavior.

EVALUATION

Criticism of Jungian therapy tends to focus on its mysticism and tendency to take social factors for granted. Even though the focus of therapy is self-discovery and not an artificial standard of normality, many Jungians pay scant attention to the political reality of people's everyday lives.

Criticism from women has centered around the archetypes as the embodiment and preservation of sexual stereotypes, since Jung postulated them as biologically and not culturally determined. Jung did work with the duality of each individual's nature, but said that a woman should not be too influenced by her animus (masculine nature), lest she be unattractive: "A woman possessed by the animus is always in danger of losing her femininity."

An inferior consciousness cannot "eo ipso" be ascribed to women; it is merely different from masculine consciousness. . . . Personal relations are as a rule more important and interesting to [a woman] than objective facts and their interconnections. The wide fields of commerce, politics, technology, and science, the whole realm of the applied masculine mind, she relegates to the penumbra of consciousness; while, on the other hand, she develops a minute consciousness of personal relationships, the infinite nuances of which usually escape the man entirely. . . . The conscious attitude of woman is in general far more exclusively personal than that of man. Her world is made up of fathers and mothers, brothers and sisters, husbands and children. . . . The man's world is the nation, the state, business concerns, etc. His family is simply a means to an end, one of the foundations of the state. . . . The general means more to him than the personal; his world consists of a multitude of coordinated factors, whereas her world, outside her husband, terminates in a sort of cosmic mist.

Jung, *Basic Writings of C.G. Jung,* p. 176–177, 180

Carl Rogers and Client-Centered Therapy

ORIGINS

Carl Rogers was born in 1902 in Oak Park, Illinois. He studied at the University of Wisconsin and New York's Union Theological Seminary. He later transferred to Columbia University for a Ph.D. in psychology. In 1942, while working at Ohio State University, Rogers wrote *Counseling and Psychotherapy: Newer Concepts in Practice,* his first book about non-directive or client-centered therapy. This was followed in 1951 by *Client-Centered Therapy: Its Current Practice, Implications, and Theory.* In 1964 Rogers left academic life for the Western Behavioral Sciences Institute in La Jolla, California.

BASIC THEORY

Client-centered therapy, which is non-analytic in approach, focuses on growth as necessary to realize the potential inherent in each person. This approach is called *client-centered* and *non-directive* because Rogers believes the function of the therapist is to support and encourage the constructive impulses within the client. The capacity for change and resolving problems is already within the client; what is crucial is the positive regard of the therapist for the client. The less the therapist thinks of her/himself as an expert, the less s/he will interfere with the client's freedom to develop the therapeutic situation to meet her own needs. Therapist and client have a warm relationship, but the dynamics of that relationship are not particularly important. Essentially, the therapist helps the client learn to live better in the world as she finds it; there is little or no emphasis on changing the environment.

Rogers sees the basic drive in human beings as the drive to self-actualization (a concept first introduced by Abraham Maslow). This is the need to grow and enhance one's experience in complex and creative ways. The person's self-concept and need for positive regard may interfere or conflict with the goal of self-actualization. The therapist, through unqualified positive regard, encourages the client to choose those experiences which enhance self-actualization. Each individual, as an infant, learns to differentiate between experiences that are self-actualizing or not; but those experiences which are self-actualizing for the client may not be met with a positive response by people in the environment, and therefore the need for a positive self-concept (as reflected by others) and the drive for self-actualization come into conflict. This is further complicated by the fact that the individual is acting on her own perceptions of reality, which may not be congruent with actual reality. The unconditional positive feelings of the therapist help to make perceptions of reality more congruent. Therapists do not interpret but may summarize and review material for the client.

TREATMENT

Since it concentrates on what the client does for herself and intervenes less in profound psychic processes, the non-directive approach is often used by guidance counselors, teachers, ministers, and others whose goal is not analytic probing, but sympathetic support of a troubled person's best impulses. Like classical psychoanalysts, non-directive therapists talk little, but for a different reason. They feel the client has the capacity to find solutions within herself if she is provided with a sympathetic listener. Non-directive therapists usually employ a face-to-face setting; they may say little, but what they say is likely to be warm and supportive. Many employ a technique known as reflecting—they mirror or paraphrase the client's statements so that the client can consider what she has really said.

EVALUATION

The limitations of Rogerian therapy stem from the unconditional positive regard of the therapist for the client. What makes client-centered therapy different from the other schools is that it leaves all responsibility for the course and direction of therapy to the client. This is fine for women who have the psychological resources to explore their own feelings, but it can be very frustrating for those who need more direction or for those with severe environmental problems (such as those centered on family or job). One of the more frustrating techniques employed by Rogerians is the one referred to—that of mirroring the client's statements. The therapist, in paraphrasing the client's statements, can sometimes be helpful by focusing what the client is talking about or feeling. But when this technique is used exclusively, it can arouse intense anger.

Rollo May and Existential Therapy

ORIGINS

Rollo May, an American analyst and existential therapist, was born in 1909 in Ohio. He was educated in Vienna and the United States, where he attended Oberlin College and the Union Theological Seminary. He received a Ph.D. from Columbia University in 1949. May worked with the William Alanson White Institute in New York, where he studied and taught analysis with many therapists from the Neo-Freudian or Cultural School. With the publication of his books *Love and Will* and *The Courage to Create,* he has become one of the leading spokespersons for existential therapy in this country.

Existential therapy differs from other schools of therapy in that there is no school or system per se. It has its roots in the philosophies of the European existentialists—Kierkegaard, Sartre, Tillich, and others—and as an analytic practice was developed by Medard Boss and Ludwig Binswanger. In this country existentialism has influenced not only Rollo May, but Abraham Maslow, Carl Rogers, and many of the therapists who usually term themselves *humanistic* or *experiential.*

BASIC THEORY

The focus of existential therapy is on the client as a *being-in-the-world*—the idea that the world and the individual are inseparable, interacting entities. Rollo May, in explaining the difference between the Freudian formulation of anxiety and the existential perception, states that Freud was describing the various *psychic mechanisms* by which anxiety is experienced and expressed, while Kierkegaard and the existential philosophers described the *experience of anxiety* as the "struggle of the living being against nonbeing." The existential therapists reject Freud's mechanistic approach to human suffering, preferring an experiential focus.

TREATMENT

Because of the lack of a system or real school, the treatment method of an existential therapist tends to vary with the therapist and her/his training and background. Since existentialists feel that the prime concern of therapy is the client's sense of alienation and despair, the focus is usually on the human loss of possibilities and the fragmentation of self rather than on childhood memories. The therapist attempts to understand the world as the client perceives it and to emphasize the values and goals of the client. The goal in therapy is to move toward self-actualization and realization of the client's potential, helping the client to find meaning in life.

Existential therapists strive for an authenticity and closeness in the therapy relationship that goes beyond the usual attachment between therapist and client but should be neither seductive nor exploitative. The existential therapist believes an objective view of the client is not really possible; s/he approaches the client with few theoretical preconceptions and deals directly with what the client reveals. Understanding the immediate meaning of the client's words is more important than looking for hidden meanings. The therapist risks reaching out to the client in the belief that the best way to help someone is not as a professional, but as a similarly vulnerable and imperfect human being.

EVALUATION

Existentialism is difficult to evaluate or criticize because of its lack of real systematization. Many therapists who sympathize with the ideas and philosophy of the existentialists may actually identify with another more specific technique, and you would need to explore with them how they integrate theory and practice. The most serious criticisms of existentialism are its lack of a theory of personality development and the extreme subjectivism of the therapist. One might also cite these two points as positive elements, since they indicate a lack of preconception about who the client is and/or should be, as well as a warm acceptance and support.

Existentialism has also been extremely influential on many other schools of therapy, particularly the experiential schools. Many existential therapists would more readily identify themselves as experiential therapists because of the emphasis on experiencing the relationship between the therapist and the client.

NOTES

1. Sigmund Freud, *A General Introduction to Psychoanalysis,* p. 21.
2. Ann Koedt, "The Myth of the Vaginal Orgasm."
3. Lucy Freeman and Julie Roy, *Betrayal.*

Chapter
5

Experiential
Therapies

In the experiential therapies the client participates actively in creating an experience for herself, rather than in analyzing past or current behavior or having such material analyzed by the therapist. The experiential therapist guides the client through her experience and sometimes structures that experience in certain ways. Each of the therapies described uses its own method of producing or structuring experience for the client, from discussion to role playing to participation in various physical exercises. Some of the experiential therapies focus directly on the active or passive manipulation of the body to deal with the physical manifestations of psychological problems. Many of these therapies also have roots in the analytic therapies, since the training of the originator was in psychoanalytic methods.

J. L. Moreno and Psychodrama

ORIGINS

J. L. Moreno was born in Rumania in 1892 and lived his early life in Vienna. He studied philosophy and theology, and finally took a degree in medicine from the University of Vienna in 1917. He was interested in drama and spontaneous dramatic play of children and made observations in these areas long before his ideas of psychodrama came into being. Moreno developed creative ideas in poetry, philosophy, theology, and literature, as well as in psychotherapy. The concepts of *here and now* and *encounter,* which were later to become so popular in the humanistic therapy movement, were originally of Moreno's invention.

From 1921 to 1923 he organized the Theater of Spontaneity in Vienna, where he began developing some of the ideas about psychodrama which he greatly expanded after his move to the United States in 1925. Although they were begun as entertainment, Moreno quickly perceived the therapeutic value of the theatrical form, recalling his earlier observations of dramatic play with children.

When he came to the United States, Moreno worked with emotionally disturbed children and further refined his ideas about psychodrama. He was concurrently developing the science of sociometry, the study of interpersonal relations within a group. Moreno emphasized the value of work with groups, and coined the term *group psychotherapy.*

In 1936 the Moreno Institute in Beacon, New York, was established as a school, a hospital, and a world center for psychodrama. Moreno married Zerka Toeman in 1949, and she and their son Jonathan worked closely with Moreno in teaching psychodrama and in editing and publishing numerous journals, books, and monographs on psychodrama, sociometry, religion, and philosophy. Since Moreno's death in 1974, they have continued his work at the Moreno Institute.

BASIC THEORY

Moreno's ideas were as numerous and as revolutionary as were Freud's, and they are now as diffused throughout popular culture. His interests covered many fields and centered on the encounter between the self and others. He saw spontaneity and creativity as primary elements in human growth; he recognized the importance of play for adults and the place it has in the growth and development of children.

The psychodramatic method is essentially existential; it attempts to deal with feelings in the here and now rather than analyzing them in the past. By re-creating important scenes from the client's life, it allows her to re-experience and examine feelings as they are occurring. The emphasis is on the client's experience of her life rather than on attempting to reach any objective view of what has happened. For this reason, fantasy, imagination, and rehearsal of alternative possibilities play a big part in psychodrama.

TREATMENT

The classical psychodrama uses five main instruments: the stage upon which the action takes place; the director, or therapist, who is responsible for helping the client keep the action moving; the client, or protagonist, who chooses the problem or area to explore; trained staff, or auxiliary egos, who play significant roles in the protagonist's drama; and the audience, or group, who may be called upon to participate in various ways. Psychodrama usually takes place in groups but has been adapted for use in numerous ways, including individual therapy.

The psychodrama begins with a warming-up process to get participants ready for action. The warm-up may consist of any of a variety of exercises involving all of the group members. For example, the director may ask the group to break into pairs and to learn something new about each other in the pair. Then pairs might join into groups of four to exchange information. By the time the whole group is reunited, each member has shared something about herself, and each member has learned something about several people. What is more important, everyone has been active in reflecting on herself and on others, sharing feelings and thoughts with others, and moving around to join other people. It is then time for the group to choose a protagonist, after which the protagonist and director explore the problem area the protagonist presents.

Then, in action, the protagonist and auxiliaries re-enact scenes of significance from the protagonist's life. The scene might begin with the re-enactment of a dream the protagonist had which involved her mother. Auxiliaries play the role of mother and anyone else in the dream. By reversing roles with the auxiliary playing her mother, the protagonist experiences a different point of view. By being allowed to confront mother in the psychodrama, the protagonist may be rehearsing for a later scene in her life, or may be examining her feelings about herself and her mother, or perhaps learning something about how she feels about herself as a mother. During the drama the protagonist may experience a strong emotional discharge or catharsis, sometimes crying or physically confronting a significant person, although not everyone experiences this discharge in the same way. The psychodrama closes with a sharing period in which members of the audience share with the protagonist and each other feelings which were aroused by the drama.

EVALUATION

Part of the essential nature of psychodrama is the control given to the protagonist. The director is there to direct the action, to help the client use a variety of methods in exploring the problem, and to keep the drama focused on the issue at hand. But the psychodrama belongs to the protagonist, and the protagonist should always retain the right to decide to stop or turn the action in a different direction. The therapist or director may guide the process of therapy, but the client or protagonist determines the content. Many people first experience psychodrama at an open demonstration in which the audience is not a screened or selected group and in which the director may never have met the protagonist before. A trained psychodramatist can handle this situation and direct a drama while keeping track of the audience experience, but a less experienced dramatist may try to show off her/his own proficiency by pushing for a dramatic catharsis when it is inappropriate.

Many therapists use bits and pieces of psychodrama technique which they have learned in workshops or in the study of other therapies. They may not even be aware that they are using psychodrama, or they may say they are psychodramatists when they have very little understanding of the processes behind the techniques. Some people may misuse psychodrama techniques for their own benefit, pushing for spectacular and showy dramas at the expense of the client. Be sure to inquire carefully about a psychodramatist's previous experience.

Although psychodrama may at times appear to produce spectacularly quick results, bypassing years of analytic therapy, the truth is that, like any real personal growth, that produced by psychodrama is gradual. Some key insights may be provided by a particular experience, and often experiential learning appears to synthesize weeks or even months of previous work; but it would be foolish to expect psychodrama to solve in one or two sessions problems that took years to build up. It often does provide a dramatic change in direction for the protagonist, however. This may be because it is the culmination of months of previous work, or because of the energy created by the group process acting as a catalyst to the individual. Often, the protagonist may return to psychodrama to re-enact or re-examine from many different perspectives the work that was done in one session.

Fritz Perls and Gestalt Therapy

ORIGINS

Frederick S. "Fritz" Perls was born in Germany in 1893 of Jewish parents, but he early renounced his religious background and became an atheist. He was interested in theater and spent some time studying it, but eventually he turned to medicine and received his M.D. in 1920. He began practice as a neuropsychiatrist and later entered therapy with Karen Horney. It was at this time that he began developing his own ideas for a new therapeutic technique. Although practicing Freudian psychoanalysis, Perls was interested in many other schools of thought and met with Wilhelm Reich to study and explore his ideas on the connection between mind and body.

Perls moved to South Africa after the Nazi presence made it impossible for him to remain in Germany, and there he developed his principles of Gestalt therapy, writing his first book, *Ego, Hunger and Aggression.* Perls remained in South Africa for twelve years, then emigrated to New York. He opened the Institute for Gestalt Therapy and wrote the definitive Gestalt text, *Gestalt Therapy,* with Paul Goodman and Ralph Hefferline. In later years, Perls spent time in residence at Esalen in California's Big Sur. He then traveled, giving lectures and demonstrations of Gestalt therapy. He died in early 1970 after a European tour. There still exist some movies of him demonstrating various kinds of Gestalt principles—movies which capture the flavor of the man and his work.

BASIC THEORY

Gestalt therapy borrows from a number of disciplines in which Perls was interested, including elements of psychodrama, body awareness, and bioenergetics, along with theoretical material from Freud and Reich. The term *Gestalt* means meaningful or coherent whole and comes from the German Gestalt psychology which studied human perception.

Perls claimed that neurosis develops when the unity of the self (which he defines as thought, feelings, and action) is split, particularly when there is an overemphasis on intellect. A result of this inner split is faulty communication between the individual and her environment. Anxiety results from the instinctive struggle for unity. For example, an individual learns as a child that expressing angry feelings is bad. As an adult, not only is she therefore unable to express anger, but she is inhibited in expressing any feelings and has trouble with intimate relationships or the enjoyment of sexuality. She is chronically anxious and has no idea why. For her the goal of therapy would be to become aware of her feelings, to integrate them into her life, and to establish a flexible interaction with her environment.

TREATMENT

Gestalt therapy focuses on the present or here and now, and the past is dealt with only as it is alive as unfinished business. Perls aimed at getting in touch with immediate needs and preferred active awareness of the present to passive reflection on the past. He insisted that people are responsible for their behavior and must take responsibility for changing (in Gestalt therapy "I can't" must be changed to "I don't want to"). He felt that people tend to project their problems onto others in order to avoid taking responsibility for change.

Gestalt technique emphasizes non-verbal experience—people talk but do not intellectualize or interpret. Therapy involves a lot of role playing or dramatization; instead of describing a relationship, the client switches chairs and pretends to be the other person. Dreams and fantasies are acted out similarly; the client pretends to be each character in her dream and comes to understand the dream through her own enactment. Clients also do awareness exercises, such as describing what they are feeling at the present moment, both emotionally and physically. Another popular exercise is to act out the split between the client's authoritative, commanding "topdog" ("You *should* do this") and her sneaky, childish "underdog" ("But I *can't!*").

Gestalt therapy is emotionally intense. The therapist is active and confrontational, especially when s/he thinks the client is playing intellectual games to avoid feeling. Therapy often takes place in workshops, where a group lives together for a weekend in order to concentrate therapy time and shorten treatment. There is little or no emphasis on how group members relate to each other or on the relationship with the therapist. People take turns working on their own issues.

EVALUATION

Gestalt therapy is of mixed value for women. On the plus side, Gestaltists value an attribute women have that society tends to undervalue—feeling. Gestalt therapy provides a permissive atmosphere in which whatever someone feels is accepted. An exception to this is the feeling of guilt. No one is allowed to feel guilty; they must understand that what they really feel is resentment. As Perls said, "The expression of resentment is one of the most important ways to help you make your life a little bit more easy." Women have so much trouble because of feeling guilty about their needs and particularly about their anger, that such encouragement can be a tremendous relief to them.

On the negative side, the anti-intellectual and confrontational nature of Gestalt leads some therapists to arrogant and contemptuous behavior. There is a fine line between therapeutic confrontation and disrespect; and not only do some therapists have trouble distinguishing between the two, but many clients are not emotionally in a position to stand up for themselves. Inexperienced therapists can also find an easy formula for doing therapy in all the various exercises, at the same time ignoring the needs of the client.

Finally, for all its talk of our alienated and lifeless society, Gestalt therapy has no theory of social psychology or human relations. As far as the Gestaltists are concerned, everything boils down to individual responsibility. The "Gestalt Prayer" reads:

I do my thing, and you do your thing.
I am not in this world to live up to your expectations
And you are not in this world to live up to mine.
You are you and I am I,
And if by chance we find each other, it's beautiful.
If not, it can't be helped.[1]

For women, this attitude completely ignores the whole issue of sex-role conditioning, sexist oppression, and the need for collective effort by all women to make social changes. Some Gestalt therapists, however, are particularly sensitive to the needs of women, and some effective therapists for women use Gestalt techniques.

Eric Berne and Transactional Analysis

ORIGINS

Eric Berne was born in 1910 and studied psychiatry and traditional psychoanalytic theory in this country. In the

1960s, deeply hurt by being denied membership in the San Francisco Psychoanalytic Institute, he developed Transactional Analysis. After the 1964 publication of his book *Games People Play,* Berne's theories gained in popularity. His work has been further popularized by Thomas Harris, who studied with Berne and wrote *I'm OK—You're OK* in 1974, soon after Berne's death in 1970.

BASIC THEORY

Berne was chiefly concerned with the length of time involved in Freudian therapy and its mystifying jargon. He felt that the theory was too complex and did not concentrate on what was important—solving people's problems.

Berne developed a system with a simplified language which is easy to understand and master in a short time. He hypothesized three parts to a person's consciousness (later refined and broken down further): the *parent,* the *adult,* and the *child.* He chose not to focus on the unconscious. The parent–adult–child are strongly reminiscent of the Freudian superego–ego–id, but are explained in simplified language that is easily understood. The parent embodies the messages, both good and bad, that the developing child heard from her own parents; the adult is the reasoning, mediating self; and the child is the natural, instinctual, playful self.

Transactions are exchanges that take place between two people and that can be analyzed as to which parts of each person's personality are taking part. *Games* are transactions with ulterior motives; and feelings of security, self-esteem, or inferiority are the *OK* or *not OK* postures. *Scripts* are the person's life plans, often not consciously thought out but embedded in early experiences.

The goal of transactional analysis is to help the client avoid self-destructive scripts, moving from playing games to intimacy. The therapist encourages the client to build a strong adult state of being. Each person should be sensitive and responsive to the child in herself.

TREATMENT

T.A. is usually conducted in small groups. It is relatively brief, often lasting for only ten to twenty weekly sessions. It is direct and pragmatic, with contracts (agreements between client and therapist about what will be worked on in therapy sessions) being decided on in early sessions. One aim is to educate the client in the T.A. language and method so that she can continue to analyze her life script without the therapy group. The therapist is an active member of the group and stays close to an equal relationship with group members. The focus of therapy is on learning how to interact effectively with other people rather than on probing inner feelings or childhood experiences.

EVALUATION

The great appeal of T.A., aside from its simple and easy-to-understand language, lies in everyone's need to feel OK. Feeling OK means being accepted and liked by peers, belonging to a group. T.A. gives you permission to be your OK self. The danger of T.A. lies in the pressure to conform to the established order of things within the group. T.A. groups are popular in corporations, prisons, the military, and other highly-structured organizations. They are used to iron out problems of relating that might develop and essentially to defuse the serious questions people are trying to raise. For example, within a banking corporation employees may practice T.A. to learn to communicate more effectively with each other or to relate to customers with complaints. They may learn to analyze interactions in terms of the other person's personality state (parent–

adult–child), but may actually overlook any serious complaint the other person is trying to express.

Even though the techniques of T.A. are essentially neutral (i.e., non-sexist and non-racist), T.A. is a spin-off of the psychoanalytic school of personality development. Therefore, sexist attitudes about female behavior may be a problem, depending on the therapist. Another development in T.A. which has attempted to address political issues is *Radical Therapy,* conceived by Claude Steiner and a group of therapists in California. Radical Therapy began as a group therapy which used T.A. language but produced a more consciously political analysis. Steiner uses the phrase *Pig Parent,* for example, as a symbol of the oppressive authority which we carry around inside us. Out of the Radical Therapy group, Hogie Wyckoff further developed and refined T.A. language to create a group therapy for women.

In her book *Solving Women's Problems,* [2] Wyckoff suggests that women, as oppressed people, have been accustomed to tuning in to other people's feelings and taking care of the unspoken needs of others. She feels that women must learn to put these skills to work for themselves, and she proposes guidelines for problem-solving groups, in which women strengthen and support each other. Problem-solving groups run along the guidelines proposed by Wyckoff can be useful to women, but they may also have some of the same drawbacks as T.A. groups. They may promote a strong group identity and a need to conform to group norms, invalidating the ideas and issues of women who disagree with group norms.

Arthur Janov and Primal Therapy

ORIGINS

Primal Therapy is the invention of Arthur Janov, an American psychologist from Los Angeles, who was trained in traditional psychoanalytic psychotherapy. In the 1960s clinical experiences with patients led Janov to develop his theory of *primal pain* and the method of unblocking it, Primal Scream Therapy. He opened the Primal Institute in Los Angeles in 1970. As the therapy developed, many of the therapists and clients involved split away to establish their own institutes, such as the Feeling Institute and the Primal Center in Kansas City.

BASIC THEORY

Janov claims that in their infancy individuals feel the need for love as well as the hurt from not receiving it, and then later in life they feel anger at having been hurt. He believes that people who are neurotic have forgotten the love and sense of pain (because of the years that have passed) and are left only with an inexplicable anger. To deal with this, Janov's theory proposes a fairly mechanistic solution, that is, the release of the primal pain through various physical exercises and, most important, through screaming. The primal trauma inflicted on the child by the parents must be dredged up and screamed out. Janov insists that his is the only way to mental health, an assertion many other therapists have made about their own methods.

TREATMENT

The goal in Primal Therapy is to unearth and release the primal pain. The client is given specific instructions and must follow them exactly. For the first phase of treatment, the client removes herself from any regular activities for several weeks, during which time she has one open-ended therapy session each day, lasting for several hours. The aim of each session is to get the client to express her deepest feelings toward her parents. To do this, she lies on the floor and attempts to get in touch with the primal pain.

She may be instructed to move her arms or legs, kicking against a pillow, in order to get the process started. She is urged to vocalize any feelings by screaming, talking baby-talk, or crying. The activity often leads to gagging, spitting, or actual vomiting, all of which is seen as release of the primal pain.

Once the client becomes accomplished in the technique, she usually joins a group. There is little interaction between clients in the therapy group, each client working out her problems individually. The therapist, or teacher, circulates in the group, working with one client at a time, encouraging clients whose efforts may be flagging. There is often considerable competition for the attention of the therapist over who is producing the best Primal.

EVALUATION

Because of its emotional intensity, Primal Therapy should be considered only by those who want to undergo extremes of experience. The goal of the therapy is emotional catharsis which may or may not have any effect on day-to-day problems of living. Primal Therapy uses extremely directive methods, with clients being ordered to make certain changes, from leaving her spouse to cutting her hair. If the client should refuse such demands or question the therapist, she is often denied further therapy.

Some clients have complained that most of the therapists (including Janov) have not experienced Primal Therapy and were in fact just testing out new ideas. In spite of this, Primal therapists claim that they have the key to mental health. In fact, many of the therapists of the Primal Institute had had only a few months of training there at the outset, and might have had very little other background in psychology. This makes the treatment extremely susceptible to abuse.

Another criticism of the Primal experience is that, like many encounter group techniques, it ignores everything but feelings, and only feelings of specific nature. Primal clients learn to focus on themselves and their feelings of pain (and perhaps to magnify that pain) and to ignore other people's feelings. They do not deal at all with the interactions of people, whether in the therapy situation or in the rest of their lives. For the Primal client her own discomfort becomes central, and relieving that discomfort (by "having a Primal") must come before everything.

Feminist Therapy

ORIGINS

Feminist Therapy is the newest of the schools of therapy we will be examining in this book. Unlike the other schools, there is no major spokesperson associated with it. Feminist Therapy is a product of the Women's Movement of the 1960s and 1970s. The need for Feminist Therapy arose from the poor treatment women had received for years from male-oriented and male-dominated schools of therapy. Most psychological theories have been proposed, developed, and practiced by men. For this reason, psychotherapy has been sexist, either in theory (e.g., Freud believed women inferior to men), or in practice (the therapist was usually a powerful male who told the female patient she should be happy as a wife and mother). Before Feminist Therapy, even women in the field of psychotherapy tended to accept male domination and sexist theories (or else they were pushed outside the mainstream of respectability).

Women who were recognizing their oppression and who were learning to demand equal rights would no longer tolerate therapy based on a double standard of mental health. Inge Broverman et al. in 1970 documented the double standard which held that a mentally healthy women (passive, dependent, non-rational) was not a mentally healthy adult (independent, assertive, logical—qualities also equated with a mentally healthy male). These standards were reflected in the attitudes and expectations of therapists (male and female) toward their clients. That study, combined with consciousness-raising about their own oppression, precipitated a change in attitudes and practice among many women who were already practicing therapists. It led to a re-examination of ideas, learned in professional training, about the limitations and expectations of women; it led to a positive approach to therapy for lesbians which said that homosexuality is a healthy and a valid lifestyle; it led to the development of a feminist therapy.

BASIC THEORY

Feminist Therapy includes an analysis of the systematic oppression of women and the ways this oppression has contributed to the problems women experience. These problems come from internal or external sources. Most schools of therapy have tended to focus on the internal sources of conflict—individual experiences, childhood trauma, problems with parents, intrapsychic conflicts that are unresolved—and to propose various ways of treating these. External sources of conflict for women have been articulated in the current Women's Movement and include: trying to fit a traditional role such as that of wife or mother; social conditioning to be passive, non-logical, "feminine," when these traits conflict with the individual's personality; overt and covert discrimination based on gender; and lack of opportunities.

Feminist Therapy deals with both the internal and the external sources of emotional problems. In therapy, this may mean active discussion of the woman's situation and oppressive elements within it, or it may mean helping women to redefine problems in a way that takes social issues into account. Rather than having a client regard her failure to gain a job promotion in purely personal terms as a lack of ability, the therapist might help her to uncover actual discrimination which has allowed few women to advance. Feminist therapists would also urge clients to join in social action with others to change the aspects of society which hold them back, rather than looking for a place to lay the blame.

The concept of androgyny has become the new model of mental health espoused by Feminist Therapy. This concept holds that there are no so-called male characteristics that only men can possess (logic, assertiveness, strength, intellect, etc.) or so-called female qualities that only women can have (sensitivity, passivity, weakness, nurturance, etc.). There is simply one spectrum of personality characteristics applicable to all people. For example, a healthy person can love babies and be good at math as well, a man may be emotional, or a woman may be logical. There is no set pattern of appropriate male and female behavior; there are only individuals.

This androgynous model automatically eliminates the double standard of mental health. All people are healthy if they are responsible and feel capable of making choices and being effective in their own lives. Because this change in therapists' attitudes toward women has taken place, there has been a corresponding change in thinking about why people have emotional problems and where these problems originate. The problems that prevent a person from feeling responsible and effective can come from either internal or external sources. Other schools of therapy have tended to focus on the internal sources of problems —individual experiences, childhood trauma, or difficulty with parents. The medical model of therapy works from the idea of "sickness" within the patient and aims at a "cure." The humanistic model aims at making people "whole" or "fulfilled," without giving adequate recognition that society creates external sources of problems. External sources, particularly for women, have only recently been defined: trying to fit a role, social conditioning, discrimination, and lack of opportunities. The socialization process creates specific problems for women. Feminist Therapy deals with both sources of emotional problems on an individual basis.

I don't know enough about Feminist Therapy. I'm sure it doesn't exclude all other matters from consideration. In some ways I resent feminism because it has made my upbringing a veritable *handicap,* something to be overcome. It has turned the world upside down. It's intellectually appealing but goes against twenty years of my thirty-year life. That's probably why I balk at Feminist Therapy. I figure it'll make me even more mixed-up than ever. I don't want to be any more "feminist" than I am now. It's made enough problems—but it's done a lot of good. I guess I'm 75 percent for feminist but 25 percent angry about it.

TREATMENT

Because Feminist Therapy is so new, it is still in the process of evolving and extending older psychological theories and techniques in order to adapt these to new ideas. Therefore, while the particular techniques of Feminist therapists may vary widely, they are always adapted to the specific needs of women. For example, a Feminist therapist who had originally been trained as a Gestalt therapist, in treating a depressed client would focus on what the client is angry about and then help her express that anger outwardly rather than directing it at herself. This is the Gestalt model. What would make this technique feminist is: (1) a sex-role analysis of how women have been conditioned not to show anger, and how that conditioning has taken place in this particular client's life, (2) sensitivity to the double challenge the client faces of overcoming both depression and social conditioning, (3) consciousness-raising with the client on the subject of women, depression, and anger, and (4) assertiveness training to enable the client to get angry in a constructive way (perhaps done in a women's group). The therapist may also suggest other resources in the community for the client, so that she may attack the sources of her depression/anger more directly when she is able. In other words, the specific technique the therapist uses to work with the client's personal issues may come from any of several schools, but will always be used in combination with sex-role analysis of women's social conditioning.

Feminist Therapy is a therapy that integrates many theories and approaches while discarding those harmful to women and all people. It incorporates psychological, social and political understandings of women's special problems and needs in an analysis of what therapy can provide for the client. It especially tries to be free from sex-based stereotypes about the way women should be and tries to allow each woman and man to make a choice.

The Feminist therapist can be a role model of a woman who values herself and other women. By valuing herself, the therapist helps the client value her own relationships with women. These may be love relationships, friendships, or relationships between colleagues, but their importance in a woman's life is recognized. Many non-feminist therapists pay attention only to the relationships women have with men and see correcting problems in those relationships as one important goal of therapy. Women have often defined the problems in their lives as revolving around the need to form a permanent relationship with a man, and this has been accepted unquestioningly by therapists as a legitimate sphere of interest. Feminist Therapy does not deny the importance for many women of relationships with men, but it does emphasize the positive aspects and importance of relationships with women. Women must also learn that their needs might be different from the needs of the men in their lives.

The goal of Feminist Therapy is to achieve a sense of effectiveness, pride, and self-respect on the part of the client, not to convert all women into politically active feminists. To achieve this, the therapist is open about her values and willing to share information about herself. She does some consciousness-raising, if the client wants it, and acts as a role model of a self-respecting woman. The therapy process itself is open for examination by the client through such techniques as contracts, negotiating of fees, learning therapy skills, and developing community resources. All this is meant to encourage in the client a sense of personal power and self-respect as a woman.

My experience with Feminist Therapy did change my ideas about the Women's Movement. It made me more aware of the underdog status of women in general and eager to become better informed on this movement, the current laws, ERA, rape, clinics, etc. For as long as I can remember I've been against racial discrimination, age discrimination, unfair treatment of the poor, etc., etc., etc. Somehow, the double standard for men and women, unfair laws, etc., never really sunk in before. Today I'm both supportive and involved with the Women's Movement.

EVALUATION

Increasing numbers of women therapists are calling themselves Feminist therapists. As with any other school of therapy, the use of this title is no guarantee of effectiveness; that will depend on the individual therapist herself. At the same time, not all women who practice this type of therapy call themselves Feminist therapists, because they prefer to identify themselves in some other way, e.g., clinical psychologist, Gestalt therapist, etc. A Feminist therapist should be willing to explain her politics, her therapy practices, and her fee scale and should be open to making contracts with her clients, encouraging in them a sense of personal power and self-worth. Feminist Therapy, however, is the only school of therapy that specifically addresses itself to the needs of women in our society, and it is for that reason that we recommend it.

Wilhelm Reich, Alexander Lowen, and Bioenergetics

ORIGINS

Bioenergetics grew out of the work of Wilhelm Reich, another Freudian dissenter. Reich split with Freud as a result of his own Marxist politics, and because he concluded from Freud's theories of sexuality that people need to experience orgasm in order to successfully resolve neurosis. Reichian analysts are now somewhat rare, possibly because Reich was a radical figure and his controversial theory and therapeutic methods provoked an extremely negative reaction in this country.

Alexander Lowen was born in the United States in 1910. Lowen began studying with Wilhelm Reich and entered Reichian therapy before he entered medical school to begin his own formal training as a psychiatrist. He was graduated from medical school in Switzerland in 1951 and returned to this country for further work with Reich and ultimately his own practice as a Reichian therapist. In 1953 Lowen and Dr. John Pierrakos launched a series of seminars which culminated in the establishment of the Institute of Bioenergetic Analysis. Lowen found himself growing further away from Reich, although he has always acknowledged his debt to him. Lowen began to feel that the emphasis that Reich put on sexuality and orgasm as the basis of human problems was too narrow and rigid; and at the same time, Reich was becoming less tolerant of disagreements. As Lowen's theories of Bioenergetics became more developed and attracted more followers, he gradually ceased to identify himself as a Reichian therapist.

BASIC THEORY

The goal of Reichian therapy is to reach the point where the client can fully express and gratify sexual needs and ultimately reach orgasm. A client in Reichian therapy generally reclines nude or semi-nude on a couch while the therapist works through the layers of muscular armor by prodding, kneading, pressing or pounding on blocked muscles until emotions are freed up. Emotions are also given verbal expression, and there is a certain amount of analysis along Freudian lines. Political discussion may also be part of the therapy.

Bioenergetics therapy, as developed by Lowen, is based on the idea that emotional problems are expressed in the body, primarily in the form of muscular tension or *body armor*. Emotional health is dependent upon the healthy functioning of the whole organism; this can be achieved only when the body energy (both emotional and muscular) can flow freely to the surface rather than be repressed. Lowen hypothesizes one basic form of energy, *bioenergy,* which can manifest itself either as psychic phenomena or physical tension. Psychoanalysis, with its primarily verbal exchange between therapist and client, does not begin to deal with these problems. Lowen felt that a new therapy was needed to facilitate the flow of bioenergy in the body and to reunite the mind and the body which have become separated through the increasing depersonalization and alienation in society.

TREATMENT

Treatment in Bioenergetic therapy is designed to unite the processes of the mind with the feelings in the body. Clients usually wear loose and comfortable clothing and do specific exercises to facilitate the acting out of these emotional processes. Therapist and client work together to locate tension, sadness, anger, or fear in the body and to unblock the flow of energy. Exercises may take the form of *stress positions* (stretching muscles to discover tension) or of working out inhibited reactions. An example of such an exercise is having the client look the therapist in the eye while repeating "no!" These activities help to increase the client's ability to express her feelings and, through increasing the consonance between the feelings and the body, increase her self-awareness and assertiveness and allow her to let go of negative feelings.

EVALUATION

Because of the involvement of the body in this therapy, women have complained that sexist therapists can make them feel worse about their bodies. Since the therapist is usually clothed and the client is in revealing clothing, she may feel uncomfortably exposed. Derogatory comments about the body may be made in the guise of therapeutic intervention. Other women have reported that Bioenergetics groups run by women have helped them learn to value and appreciate their bodies and to feel more at ease with themselves. Some combine Bioenergetics with a more verbal form of therapy. One goal of Bioenergetics is to feel comfortable with, and to like, your body, which is certainly a specific need of women.

NOTES

1. Frederick S. Perls, *Gestalt Therapy Verbatim,* p. 4.
2. Hogie Wyckoff, *Solving Women's Problems.*

Chapter

6

Behavior Therapies

Behavior therapies are those which focus on changing behavior in clients rather than on seeking out the causes of such behavior and attempting to change the circumstances (intrapsychic or social) which gave rise to the behavior. There is an emphasis on various kinds of behavior as ineffective and problematic, and in general a goal of the therapies is eliminating that behavior. This might include problems as diverse as a crippling phobia which does not allow a person to leave the house, a habit (and possible addiction) such as cigarette smoking, and socially unacceptable habits of some former mental patients (such as accosting strangers on the street or begging for cigarettes).

Behavior Modification

ORIGINS

In 1912 the psychologist John Watson proposed behaviorism as the scientific approach to the modification and control of behavior. His early work defined the science and spelled out the principles of learning theory, but B. F. Skinner (leading American behaviorist, born in 1904) contributed major ideas to our present knowledge and use of behavior modification as therapy today. In 1938, with the publication of *Behavior of Organisms,* Skinner proposed a system for distinguishing normal, neurotic, and psychotic behavior, thereby coming to prominence in the field. He suggested reward as a major factor in shaping behavior, since a person rewarded for a specific act tends to repeat that act. Behavior which goes unrewarded is gradually extinguished. Activity must be broken down into easily performed, separate steps (behaviors), and the person can be rewarded (reinforced) for each step until a complex task is mastered. In this way, through the manipulation of rewards, behavior can be shaped and controlled. Skinner's book *Walden Two* (1948), about a behaviorally engineered Utopian society, expresses the principles of positive reinforcement.

BASIC THEORY

The purpose of behavior modification is to help the client break habits or extinguish behavior that is not useful. To do this, the therapist must discover the existing behavior patterns and help to remove any reinforcement that perpetuates the undesirable behavior. Depending on the severity of the problem, modification can be achieved either independently or under the guidance of a therapist.

Behavior modification differs radically from any of the other schools of therapy we have discussed because the primary focus is on changing behavior and not on increasing the client's awareness of or insight into herself. The behaviorists feel that increased self-esteem and self-confidence are a *result* of learning new patterns of behavior; other schools of therapy tend to feel that self-understanding will *produce* those changes. Perhaps the only answer to this "which comes first" question is, again, whichever feels right to the individual.

TREATMENT

The behavior therapist begins by defining existing patterns of behavior. S/he then proceeds to eliminate the reinforcements which support the undesirable behavior and provides motivation to change the behavior. The client needs to have an incentive to change and must be realistic about setting achievable goals. Treatment often begins by having the client keep a notebook, recording in it instances of the behavior which is to be changed. If the client wants to stop smoking, for example, she may keep a record of how many cigarettes she smokes, when she smokes them, and what feelings smoking involves. Only after she has made this record does the therapist help her devise a systematic plan to reward her not smoking and to eliminate the rewards for smoking.

Another behavior modification technique is called *systematic desensitization.* This is a relaxation process used to eliminate specific fears. For example, if a client is afraid of public speaking, she is first instructed in relaxation. Then she is instructed to imagine, or participate in, situations which cause her anxiety. The therapy starts from the situation which causes the least anxiety (perhaps answering a question in class) and proceeds gradually to the situation which previously caused the most anxiety (such as lecturing to a large audience). Whether done in imagination or in actual experience, each new step is undertaken only after no more fear of the previous one remains. Phobias are often treated this way.

Operant conditioning, or the rewarding of desired behavior, has been proved effective in institutional settings with autistic children, retarded people, and some mental patients, since these populations are not in control of their environment. The therapist or staff member is able to effectively manipulate the rewards available in the institutional environment surrounding these patients and can provide strong incentives for change, since they are often using very basic rewards such as food, attention, and privileges. In situations where the population is functioning at a higher or more sophisticated level, administering such a program is more difficult. This has been used in prisons and mental hospitals where all privileges (eating meals with other inmates, taking a shower, having visitors, or being allowed to wear non-institutional clothes) are denied until the inmate cooperates by behaving in the desired way. In some institutions participants are given a token of some sort for each small act of desired behavior. Tokens can be accumulated and later exchanged for a particular reward such as food or TV privileges. These are referred to as *token economies.*

Aversion therapy is another form of behavior modification which involves punishing undesirable behavior. This is a very controversial therapy because of the punishments involved. One technique commonly used with alcoholics consists of giving medication which makes the person violently ill when alcohol is consumed. Another technique is to pair the sight of a drink (or for homosexuals, the sight of an attractive, same-sex person) with an electric shock. In prisons, the drug Anectine has been used in aversion therapy. Jessica Mitford, in her book *Kind and Usual Punishment,* reports: "According to Dr. Arthur Nugent, chief psychiatrist at Vacaville (prison) and an enthusiast for the drug, it induces 'sensations of suffocation and drowning.' The subject experiences feelings of deep horror and terror, 'as though he were on the brink of death.' While he is in this condition, the therapist scolds him for his misdeeds and tells him to shape up or expect more of the same."[1]

EVALUATION

Behavior modification is most successful in treating specific problems which can be broken down into discrete behaviors that are worked on step by step, such as phobias or bedwetting or some sexual problems. This approach is not so helpful with generalized depression or dissatisfaction with life, however. Often behaviorists try to break these less specific problems down into a series of steps. They may succeed in part but ignore some of the additional feelings which accompany the symptoms or stop looking any further once they have found one issue that can be treated behaviorally. If you are considering behavior therapy, you must decide for yourself whether you want to simply change a certain behavior or gain a deeper understanding of yourself.

We feel that behavior therapy is a tool that can be used as an adjunct to psychotherapy. You must give consent to its use, and you have the right to know at all times what is going on and why, so that you can modify or withdraw from the procedure at any time. The problem with behavior therapy is that it is often misused on people who are incapable of giving informed consent, such as the retarded, children, and inmates of prisons and mental hospitals.

William Glasser and Reality Therapy

ORIGINS

William Glasser is an American psychiatrist who was born in 1925 and is now practicing in Los Angeles. Toward the end of his psychiatric training he developed Reality Therapy because he felt that other therapies were ineffective. He has established an Institute for Reality Therapy in Los Angeles, and some of the ideas of Reality Therapy have been popularized by his books, *The Identity Society* and *Reality Therapy*.

BASIC THEORY

Central to Reality Therapy are the three Rs: reality, responsibility, and right-and-wrong. The goals of Reality Therapy are to face reality, or the world around you, accept responsibility for your behavior, and learn to behave correctly. The therapist's tools are morality and discipline. Clients are expected to learn how to behave responsibly, that is, conform to established order.

Glasser contends that no matter what the problem is, from nervous headaches to delusions about who you are, the common cause is the inability to fulfill two essential needs: to love and be loved, and to feel worthwhile to ourselves and others. Those who are unable to fulfill these needs in themselves are characterized by Glasser as irresponsible. Because he does not accept the term "mental illness," Glasser feels that he does not allow the client to evade responsibility for her own behavior or for changing it in order to be more productive.

TREATMENT

The essential aspect of Reality Therapy is the relationship between the client and the therapist. Glasser maintains that therapists must themselves be responsible people and be willing to discuss their lives openly with clients. A Reality therapist should understand and accept the client as she is, so that the therapist may guide her to satisfy her needs in the real world.

The focus in this therapy is on the behavior of the client rather than on attitude. If behavior changes, it is assumed that attitudinal changes will follow. There is little or no focus on the past, which is not open to change, and Glasser does not allow it to be an excuse or explanation for present behavior.

EVALUATION

Reality Therapy has been popular in prisons, reform schools, and some mental hospitals—at least with the staff. Some therapists feel better when they can take a stance of moral correctness, and some clients may feel better when they can obey the moral imperatives of an authority and thus feel secure in being acceptable to the community. We believe this is a dangerous guise for helping people judged to be social deviants to adjust to the status quo. For women struggling to break out of stereotyped roles, Reality Therapy could be disastrous.

Albert Ellis and Rational Emotive Therapy

ORIGINS

Albert Ellis, an American psychologist, was born in 1913 in Pittsburgh, Pennsylvania. He studied at Columbia University and has taught extensively in the New York area. In his work with the Institute for Rational Living, he developed *A Guide to Rational Living* with Robert Harper. This was later expanded in *Rational Psychotherapy* and *Handbook of Psychotherapies.* His guidelines were based on the idea that you can lead a fulfilling and satisfying life if your thinking is organized and disciplined.

BASIC THEORY

Ellis devised a method of self-analysis which is based on controlling thoughts and the emotions associated with them. This is done by putting the emotions into formalized sentences and then analyzing the message in the sentence. The person then substitutes more rational statements for the irrational and useless ones. People may believe, for example, that they should be competent, adequate, and achieving in all respects. This idea may be reinforced by parents or by unrealistic social expectations. Rational

Emotive Therapy would have the person examine rationally whether these expectations are realistic and concentrate on the messages that tell one that it is possible to lead a fulfilling life without being perfect in every respect.

TREATMENT

The basic premise of Rational Emotive Therapy is that your ability to reason can help you achieve a satisfying emotional existence. In a very direct and confrontational manner, the therapist teaches the client to eliminate depression, guilt, or anger by thinking straight and taking effective action. Clients must learn how their thinking patterns are self-defeating and assess their value systems. For example, believing that you must be competent and successful in all respects is irrational and can lead to self-hatred; the Rational Emotive therapist would help you evaluate real priorities and form realistic expectations.

EVALUATION

As a method of self-analysis, Rational Emotive Therapy offers a "power of positive thinking" road to comfort and is not harmful, but as a therapy technique we feel that the technique of authoritative confrontation contradicts the goal of self-responsibility and leads to intellectualizing.

Hypnosis in Therapy, or Hypnotherapy

ORIGINS

Hypnosis has been used for many years as part of the treatment of psychological or emotional problems. Freud experimented with it in the late 1890s, but discarded it in favor of his own approach to the unconscious—psychoanalysis. Hypnosis is one of the many skills a therapist might use during treatment. It is not so much a therapy as a capacity to induce a trance state in one's self by concentration.

The focus of hypnotherapy is on removing or alleviating a specific symptom. This may be a tic or a paralysis, a state of insomnia, or an asthma attack. The client not only experiences relief because the symptom is gone, but she may feel she has more control over herself as a result of learning relaxation and self-hypnosis techniques. Hypnosis is particularly useful in the control of pain when a client is unable or unwilling to use drugs.

Hypnosis is a state of altered consciousness in which the subject narrows and focuses the field of concentration. This trance state can be induced in response to a signal from another person or from oneself. The usual means of inducing hypnosis is to focus attention with repetitive suggestion ("You feel your eyes closing; you are feeling tired") or by having the subject concentrate on a visual point.

Some psychoanalysts still use hypnosis in the way Freud did, to gain access to the client's unconscious thoughts. In other therapies, the client's passive state in the hypnotic trance is used for active counter-suggestion by the therapist. For example, "When you wake up, you will no longer feel the desire to smoke." Often clients hear suggestions like these in a group setting where several clients are in a trance, or relaxed state, at the same time.

In other situations, the client may learn to induce the trance state herself in order to exercise control over undesirable symptoms, such as anxiety or asthma attacks. The client learns to relax, close her eyes, and concentrate on being relaxed and comfortable. She also learns a signal, such as letting one arm rise, which indicates to her that she is comfortably in a trance. She then gives herself suggestions about the lessening or removal of symptoms. For example, an asthmatic client may repeat (aloud or to herself), "I am breathing comfortably, I am taking slow, deep breaths, I do not feel short of breath." She may then leave the state of relaxation. The client practices these techniques several times with the therapist and then practices frequently by herself outside the sessions until she feels confident that she can use this technique when she needs it.

EVALUATION

Hypnotherapy has limited application. Although it has been used to temporarily alleviate incapacitating symptoms such as paralysis, tics, or amnesia so a client may work psychotherapeutically to determine the causes of the symptoms, drugs are more often used today for these purposes. Hypnosis has also been used as a shortcut to break unwanted habits, such as smoking or overeating; but hypnosis by itself has no permanent psychotherapeutic effects, and the habit may reappear unless other measures are taken.

The success of hypnotherapy depends on the client's receptivity and ability to concentrate, and on her willingness to assume a state of mind in which mature discriminations are suspended. We believe this renunciation of self-responsibility to a powerful authority figure is particularly detrimental to women. If you are considering hypnotherapy, we urge you to do so in conjunction with psychotherapy and to be particularly aware of the value system of the hypnotherapist. Try to find a hypnotherapist who teaches self-hypnosis, which is used for relaxation prior to procedures such as dentistry, or which may be taught to help control life-threatening problems such as asthma. Self-hypnosis can be a valuable tool in the exercise of control over one's life.

NOTES

1. Jessica Mitford, *Kind and Usual Punishment,* p. 140.

Chapter 7

Medical Therapy and Drugs

Medical therapy—the use of psychotropic (mood-altering) drugs (or chemotherapy), electroconvulsive therapy (shock, or ECT), and psychosurgery—is more widely used in treating emotional problems than any other form of therapy. Medical treatment, like behavior modification, is aimed at alleviating symptoms. Drugs, shock treatment, or psychosurgery *do not cure* emotional problems. They control symptoms and, in addition, they often produce debilitating side effects.

We obviously recommend psychotherapy (of many varieties) as a helpful approach to alleviating mental stress; but we do feel that the limited use of some of the various drug treatments can be a helpful adjunct to psychotherapy.* This would apply to people who are simply too agitated or depressed to respond to verbal therapy. We would

*The debate over actual causes of emotional or mental problems has raged for years. It is not within the scope of this book to compare such theories as chemical imbalance (megavitamin therapy), genetics, or the whole nature/nurture question.

not recommend electroshock treatment or psychosurgery except in the direst of circumstances and never without careful consultation and consideration of alternatives.

We are strongly opposed to the therapeutic approach, used by many psychiatrists and other physicians, which makes chemotherapy the major treatment and ignores the other needs of the patient. Drugs and shock treatment are incredibly abused by some doctors to increase their income and keep bothersome patients under control.[1] Some physicians use these means to conceal their own anxiety or lack of skill when confronted by emotionally-disturbed people. Because these therapists are primarily doctors (the only therapists empowered to administer drug treatment and electroshock), they lend this approach an air of authority, and because the techniques are medical, people subjected to them accept the mystifying aspects without too much question. We are used to having doctors diagnose an illness and prescribe a treatment for it, and to following her/his instructions without many questions, expecting a "cure."

Clients must question the use of any medical treatments, and such treatments should not be given without informed consent. For consent to any treatment to be considered informed, it must be given voluntarily, the person giving it must be competent to make such a decision, and there must be an understanding of what the intended treatment consists of, both the positive and negative effects. Thus, decisions about the use of drugs, psychosurgery, or electroshock treatment should not be made in a matter of minutes, but only after careful consideration. It is important for people faced with decisions about medical treatment to realize that doctors and scientists themselves are not clear about how and why these techniques work, if and when they actually do work. Research into the workings of the brain is still in its infancy; even so, the work that has been done is complicated and technical, and its findings are subject to many different interpretations by different experts.

We are not saying that drugs or surgery may not help or cure identifiable brain diseases or neurological syndromes. Nor are we suggesting that acute symptoms such as suicidal depression or overwhelming anxiety shouldn't be thus alleviated. The problem lies with any therapist's *exclusive* reliance on these methods, rather than on a use of them as an aid to help the client reach a stage at which she can better deal with problems in her life. Drugs can be used to reduce excessive anxiety or depression to the point where serious psychotherapeutic work becomes possible. Unfortunately, they may also reduce the motivation to do this work, because the senses are dulled and the symptoms under control.

Overuse of Medical Treatment

Forty-three percent of all adults in the United States today use tranquilizers and/or other doctor-prescribed mood-changing drugs—more than half of these women.[2] Why is medical treatment more common than any other therapy for emotional problems? One answer is that drugs are big business. Drug companies spend thousands of dollars on advertising to promote their particular brands of drugs and give doctors free samples, persuasive literature, notepads, and desk sets stamped with brand names, and other more expensive promotional items. Drugs and ECT also take less time than psychotherapy; they lift the weight of responsibility for dealing with underlying problems off both the client and the therapist.

Another answer is politics. Medical treatments have been used as a means of what is known as chemical restraint in mental institutions and prisons with those classified as depressed, hyperactive, and aggressive; they have essentially replaced the straitjacket and the padded cell (it is less expensive to use drugs than to add more staff). Any situation in which the patients involved are not valued by society and in which they have been gathered in large numbers under the control of only a few attendants contributes to an expanding market for drug companies; witness the use of the drug Ritalin in treating hyperactive or other children, when there may be strong arguments that their problems are caused by overcrowded, understaffed schools, rather than by the individual children themselves.

Addiction and overdose more commonly result from the abuse of prescribed drugs than from the use of illegal drugs.* This is the result of the manufacture of greater quantities of drugs than are actually prescribed, the promotion of drugs by the pharmaceutical companies without sufficient warning or information given as to side effects and the dangers of using more than one drug at a time, and the ease with which these drugs are prescribed by physicians too lazy or too overworked to alert their patients to the dangers involved.

Psychoactive Drugs

MAJOR TRANQUILIZERS

Imagine this scene: You are in a locked ward of a mental hospital. Some patients are wandering the halls with a slow, shuffling gait and a blank look on their faces. One man is asleep on the floor; several others have been sitting in front of the TV for hours, watching nothing. The smell of urine indicates that someone has been incontinent. One woman makes slow, rhythmical movements with her mouth—protruding her tongue, smacking her lips, blow-

---

*The National Institute on Drug Abuse estimates that sleeping pills are associated with nearly 5,000 deaths a year and cause another 50,000 trips to emergency rooms and drug abuse centers (*New England Magazine, The Boston Globe,* July 30, 1978).

ing out her cheeks, and moving her chin from side to side.

Are these the bizarre symptoms of madness? Not at all. Every one of these people is exhibiting the effects of the major tranquilizers—Thorazine, Stellazine, Mellaril, or Haldol.* Over 250 million people have taken these drugs since their introduction in the mid-1950s. Although a single dose of any antipsychotic drug is seldom dangerous, the continued administration of these drugs over a period of weeks or months can cause serious complications. Tardive dyskinesia, a disease of the nervous system indicated by the mouth movements of the woman described above, is one possible side effect. Once it has developed fully, it is irreversible, even after drug therapy is discontinued.[3] If the physician is alert to initial symptoms (wormlike movements of the tongue) and medication is discontinued, the full syndrome may not appear.[4] The necessary vigilance is often lacking, though, especially for those patients to whom the drug is given on an out-patient basis and who see a busy or bored doctor once a month simply for the renewal of the drug prescription. Although definitive studies of the effects of the syndrome on intelligence and emotions have not been conducted, pathological studies indicate that the neurological damage to the brain is irreversible.[5]

According to Dr. George Crane, clinical professor of psychiatry at the University of North Dakota School of Medicine, "the large doses of neuroleptic drugs that are now prescribed by most psychiatrists are not only harmful but also unnecessary. . . . The number of neurological disorders can only increase if current practices of antipsychotic drug use are allowed to continue."[6] Dr. Crane reached his conclusions when he discovered that six months after he

*The drug companies would prefer to call these "side effects." These may not be the actions for which the drugs are prescribed, but they are still important effects.

had lectured on the dangers of high dosages of neuroleptic drugs in eight representative psychiatric wards, the average daily dose of the drugs had *increased.*

Other side effects that may accompany the use of the major tranquilizers are acute dystonic reactions (bizarre, involuntary contractions of muscles, which may take the form of grimacing, facial tics, jerking arms and legs, open mouth, protruding tongue, eyes fixed and rotated laterally), akathisias (restlessness and inability to sit still, strange feelings in the extremities), and Parkinsonian syndrome (weakness, fatigue, or tremors, masklike face, and rigidity). These side effects may be treated with still more drugs (often Artane or Cogentin) which bring with them their own side effects (blurred vision, constipation, dry mouth, mild hypertension). Some of these symptoms can be painful and confusing, seriously complicating the life of the person taking the drugs and leading them to feel it is part of their illness.

Tranquilizers helped immediately, but they didn't explain why I was feeling pain or show me how to deal with it!

Tranquilizers helped reduce my anxiety, depression, and insomnia so I got through a year of teaching. But I was very glad to get off them and *feel alive* again. I have resisted taking them ever since.

I was prescribed mild tranquilizers but I stopped taking them because they made me feel that I was unable to control my own mind.

MINOR TRANQUILIZERS

By far more commonly prescribed, the minor tranquilizers include Librium, Valium (the single most prescribed drug), Equanil, and Miltown. Many women have been taking these drugs regularly for years to cope with such problems as chronic depression or anxiety. The most common side effects are drowsiness, fatigue, and lack of muscular coordination. If used in conjunction with alcohol or any of a variety of other drugs, these tranquilizers enhance the effect of the alcohol or other drug, rendering the patient unable to make judgments about how much she has had to drink or which drugs she has actually taken. People taking these drugs are warned not to drive or use machinery (although many who are accustomed to the drugs ignore these warnings at great risk to themselves and others), so that it effectively cuts down on their ability to work. Prolonged use may lead to various problems of physical addiction (especially with Miltown), and abrupt withdrawal can be painful. The symptoms of withdrawal include anxiety, irritability, and vomiting.

ANTIDEPRESSANTS

The antidepressants include tricyclics (Elavil and Tofranil), and the monoamine oxidase or MAO inhibitors (Marplan, Parnate, Nardil). These drugs work on enzyme reactions in the body. The tricyclics relieve depression through a sedative effect, although how they actually work is not known. They usually take up to several weeks to begin to have an effect. Dry mouth and blurred vision are common side effects, as well as dizziness or faintness. The MAO inhibitors are used less often since they require close medical supervision. They are more likely to be used on a long-term basis. They often do have a seemingly miraculous effect in the relief of severe depression, but they are used less often than the tricyclics because, in combination with certain foods (including chocolate, cheese, raisins, and certain fish) and common medications, they can cause a serious rise in blood pressure.

AMPHETAMINES

Amphetamines, commonly referred to as "speed" or "uppers" (including Benzadrine and Dexadrine), are stimulants which can make you feel mildly euphoric and energetic and suppress your appetite. Because you develop a tolerance to these drugs, needing ever-increasing doses to get the same effect, they are considered addictive. Long-term use can damage the central nervous system, cause paranoia or unwarranted suspiciousness, or sometimes produce psychotic symptoms. Short-term side effects include nervousness, poor judgment, insomnia, rapid heartbeat, and even extreme aggressiveness.

In previous years amphetamines were widely prescribed for weight control and were treated very casually. Users who did not know what drug they were taking or did not understand its effects could become addicted or fall into a pattern of multiple drug use. They would take amphetamines to suppress appetite, then a tranquilizer or alcoholic drink to calm the jumpiness caused by the amphetamines. If they used tranquilizers or sleeping pills at night, they would need to take another amphetamine in the morning "to get going." These drugs are extremely dangerous in combination with each other or with alcohol because of their unpredictable interactions.

Because amphetamines have an opposite effect on children who have not reached puberty (calming them down instead of increasing their energy), they are sometimes prescribed to control hyperactivity or for children diagnosed as minimally brain-damaged (MBD). Prescribing a drug is a quick, cheap, and effective method of controlling behavior. It would be preferable to consider the possible social causes of hyperactivity, such as over-crowded classrooms, poor nutrition, and lack of sufficient or interesting classroom materials. The long-term effects of amphetamine use on children are not known.

LITHIUM

Lithium differs from other mood-changing medications because it is not a drug, but a mineral which occurs in nature in the form of a salt. It is administered in tablet or capsule form as Lithium Carbonate USP, Eskalith, Pfi-Lithium, Lithane, Lithonate, and Lithotabs. The action of lithium is not clearly understood. It is used to treat manic episodes of manic-depressive illness and appears to level out the intensity of the mood swings. Recently it has been prescribed more frequently and has sometimes been inappropriately prescribed for depression, in which cases its effectiveness may be limited.

Lithium is a dangerous medication and carries the warning, "Lithium toxicity is closely related to serum lithium levels and can occur at doses close to therapeutic levels. Facilities for prompt and accurate serum lithium determination should be available before initiating therapy."[7] This means that a dose slightly above the normal dose (which varies from person to person) may be poisonous. Patients who are taking lithium must have blood samples taken and monitored closely, especially when they first use it, since their dosages may have to vary. Lithium side effects include hand tremors, thirst, nausea, fatigue, slurred speech, or muscle weakness.

Brand Names of Commonly Prescribed Psychotropic Drugs

For further information on the contraindications and side effects of any of the drugs listed on page 102, check the *Physicians' Desk Reference* at your library.

ANTIPSYCHOTIC AGENTS OR MAJOR TRANQUILIZERS

Phenothiazine Derivatives		*Thioxanthene Derivatives*	*Other Agents*
Thorazine	Stelazine	Taractan	Haldol
Vesprin	Trilafon	Navane	Moban
Sparine	Proketazine		Loxitane
Mellaril	Tindal		
Serentil	Repoise		
Quide	Prolixin		

ANTIANXIETY AGENTS OR MINOR TRANQUILIZERS

Benzodiazepines	*Propanediols*
Librium	Equanil
Valium	Miltown
Serax	Solacen
Tranxene	Tybatran
Ativan	
Dalmane	

ANTIDEPRESSANT AGENTS

Tricyclics		*Monamine Oxidase Inhibitors (MAOI)*	*Other Agents*
Tofranil	Aventyl	Marplan	Deprol
Presamine	Vivactil	Nardil	Etrafon
Pertofrane	Sinequan	Parnate	Triavil
Norpramin	Adapin		
Elavin			

PSYCHOSTIMULANTS

Amphetamine and Amphetamine-like Stimulants

Benzadrine	Dexadrine
Desoxyn	Methadrine
Ritalin	Cylert

Shock Treatment (ECT)

Electro-Convulsive Therapy, or shock treatment, was introduced in the 1930s and widely hailed as a new cure-all for emotional disorders. After the introduction of psychotropic drugs in the 1950s, the use of ECT declined, and most responsible psychiatric texts recommend it as a treatment only for severe, life-threatening depression that has not responded to drug therapy. There is still wide debate over the use of ECT on schizophrenics.

HOW DOES ECT WORK?

ECT consists of a series of six to ten treatments on successive days, and a series may be repeated after a short interval. Electrodes are placed on the patient's head, a conducting paste or jelly is applied, and a *grand mal* convulsion is induced by passing a small current of electricity (300 to 1,200 milliamperes at 70 to 130 volts) through the brain for a brief period of time (current is built up over a ten-second period and sharply decreased when the convulsion has occurred).[8] The patient is first anesthetized and then given an injection of succinylcholine (Anectine, Sucostrin), a derivative of curare. The succinylcholine paralyzes the muscles, relaxing them almost instantly, thereby allowing the convulsion to occur without the stiffening and spasmodic jerking which formerly accompanied ECT. Before this drug came into use, patients were held down by attendants during the convulsion, and injuries, even fractures, were not uncommon. When succinylcholine is used, patients must be given oxygen for several minutes immediately following the treatment, until spontaneous respiration occurs, and treatment should *never* be given without the aid of a trained anesthetist and the ready availability of facilities for oxygen treatment and respiration.[9] Following the treatment, patients sleep and then are allowed to eat after an hour or so. Patients almost always sustain immediate memory loss, some confusion and disorientation, and may complain of headache or other pain.

No one is clear as to why inducing a *grand mal* seizure has the effect of relieving severe depression, but clinical tests have shown that it does work. It does not prevent the recurrence of depression, however, and is not a cure. Again, most physicians would prescribe ECT only when a patient has not responded to psychotherapy, psychotropic drugs, or when the depression is so severe the patient's life appears to be endangered. Unfortunately, there are psychiatrists or physicians who use ECT as a substitute for therapy and appear to prescribe it almost routinely for a majority of their patients. This indiscriminate use allows them to treat large numbers of patients in a short time and yields high fees. ECT also has the effect of appearing to satisfy the demands of the patient's family. Often, psychotherapy is regarded as "doing nothing" or "just talking," and impatient family members want a more speedy recovery.

Both the effects of ECT and the sensations that occur during treatment are in dispute. Physicians often insist that there is no permanent memory loss from ECT, but many patients claim that there is a permanent loss of memory not only of events but also of previously held skills.[10] Some doctors say that ECT may result in subtle brain damage and that they have several patients with histories of good intelligence who had subnormal IQ tests after ECT. Other doctors deny this and assert that brain damage may have occurred only as a result of improper administration of oxygen during treatment.[11] Doctors also claim that there is little discomfort associated with the treatment and convulsion, now that succinylcholine is used; patients still maintain, however, that the confusion and discomfort on awakening is also sometimes accompanied by pain during the actual treatment.

Certainly, ECT is a treatment which should not be lightly undertaken by anyone. If you are a voluntary patient in a hospital, you can refuse to sign consent forms for the treatment; involuntary patients may need additional legal help to block its use. Don't agree to sign for the ECT treatment of a relative until you have thoroughly explored other avenues and sought a second opinion. If the doctor who is treating you or a relative will not consider such a consultation, you should seek the advice of another therapist.

Psychosurgery

Psychosurgery refers to operations on healthy brain tissue for the purpose of changing the behavior, emotional reactions, or personality characteristics of a person. In this procedure, healthy tissue is destroyed by removal, searing, or electrical stimulation, or nerve pathways are severed in order to change the functioning of the brain and consequently the person's behavior. Psychosurgery is an extremely serious operation—it is a *permanent* alteration of the brain, and the effects are *irreversible.* The exact effects are unpredictable, as they vary from person to person, and since the procedures are still experimental, long-term follow-up studies have not yet been done. Any definitive data come from animal studies; but no adequate comparison can be drawn between docility in monkeys and blunted emotions or creativity in human beings.

Prefrontal lobotomy, which was the most common psychosurgery performed in the 1950s (estimates are made that over 50,000 were performed), involves cutting some of the nerve pathways to the frontal lobe of the brain. Lobotomies were often performed on committed patients without their consent. Dr. Karl Pribram of Stanford, a specialist in brain function, recalls the "heyday of psychosurgery, when frontal lobotomy was an accepted routine procedure. Psychiatrists would certify a patient for surgery. ... Often surgeon and patient did not become acquainted until after the operation when dressings had to be changed."[12] Permanent side effects are common, including loss of motivation to work hard at anything, lack of ability to plan for the future, and deterioration of ordinary social habits.

Since the 1960s lobotomies have been replaced by the cingulotomy, ambyglotomy, and other equally risky operations with more scientific-sounding names, which can also have drastic effects on behavior. These operations have been used to control "aggression" in prison inmates and mental patients, and also to control hyperactivity in children. Because psychosurgery is a form of behavior control and has the effect of blunting active behavior if carried out extensively enough, there is a temptation to use it for non-therapeutic purposes. Consider a violent prison inmate, for example. Her violence may be a philosophically appropriate response to her repressive situation, or even an expression of her political views, but the prison authorities who work with her may view such violence as irrational and sick. Thorazine and psychosurgery can be, and are, used to control or punish obstreperous inmates.[13]

Even though psychosurgery cannot be performed without the consent of the patient or legal guardian (who may be the state), there is no legal protection of the rights of the patients provided by special review procedures. In March, 1977, the National Commission for the Protection of Human Subjects of Biomedical and Behavioral Research issued recommendations on psychosurgery, but the Secretary of Health, Education, and Welfare has yet to implement them. If psychosurgery is legally defined as an experimental process, this will provide much needed public safeguards and protect people from involuntary surgery for behavioral control.

Guidelines for Medical Treatment

• *When interviewing a therapist, ask what her/his opinions are on medication or ECT and whether s/he ever recommends these forms of treatment.* Therapists who routinely prescribe drugs are less likely to be skilled in psychotherapy, since they often rely on the drugs to solve the patient's problem.

• *Do not consent to medication just because a therapist or doctor tells you it is necessary.* As in any form of therapy, you should agree to medication only if it makes sense to you. *The decision is yours.* You have a right to a second opinion, particularly if the therapist prescribes more than a minor tranquilizer. Many therapists want you to take medication because they are uncomfortable with your anxiety, but the issue is what *you* want to do.

• *Find out all the possible side effects before you accept any medication.* This information is available in the *Physicians' Desk Reference,* which you can find in most public libraries. Ask the doctor for the literature accompanying the drug. Many therapists and doctors take the attitude that side effects from drugs are statistically improbable, and that the therapeutic results are worth the risk. Do not accept this attitude unless you have fully considered all the alternatives and weighed the possible consequences. *You* should be the one to determine how much risk you want to take with your body.

• *Medical treatment must be prescribed in conjunction with a complete medical checkup.* The prescribing physician (whether a psychiatrist or your own regular physician) should be aware of any medical problems, allergies, or drug reactions you have, as well as any other medications you are taking.

• *As a general rule, avoid taking any such medication while pregnant.* If you are pregnant, these treatments may have disastrous consequences for your child. You should consult your obstetrician first before consenting to take any medication while pregnant.

NOTES

1. Thomas Kiernan, *Shrinks, etc.,* p. 247.

2. Ibid, p. 250.

3. Ellen L. Bassuk, M.D., and Steven C. Schoonover, M.D., *The Practitioner's Guide to Psychoactive Drugs,* pp. 92–3.

4. George E. Crane, M.D., "The Prevention of Tardive Dyskinesia," *American Journal of Psychiatry,* 134:7, July 1977, p. 757.

5. Peter Schrag, *Mind Control,* p. 110.

6. Crane, "Tardive Dyskinesia."

7. *Physicians' Desk Reference,* 31st ed. (Ordell, N.J.: Charles E. Baker, Jr., 1977), p. 1258.

8. A. H. Chapman, *Textbook of Clinical Psychiatry* (Philadelphia: Lippincott, 1978), pp. 441–5.

9. *Physicians' Desk Reference,* p. 675–6.

10. Cyril Athana Kolocotronis, "The Truth about Electro-Shock Treatments," *Madness Network Reader,* Sherry Hirsch, et al., eds., p. 87.

11. Fred H. Frankel, Chairman, "Electro-Convulsive Therapy in Massachusetts: A Task Force," *Massachusetts Journal of Mental Health,* vol. III, No. 2, Winter 1973, pp. 4–5.

12. Karl Pribram, M.D., "Autism: A Deficiency in Context-Dependent Processes?," *Research and Education: Proceedings of the Second Annual Meeting and Conference of the National Society for Autistic Children,* C. C. Park, ed. (Washington, D.C.: NIMH: Public Service Publication No. 2164, 1971).

13. Mitford, *Kind and Usual Punishment,* pp. 140–1.

Part III

Getting Help

Chapter
8

Adjuncts and Alternatives to Therapy

Adjuncts to Therapy

There are many specialized adjuncts to therapy with which you might have contact—usually as a useful addition to a therapy program, but sometimes as your primary therapy. These adjuncts are: Occupational Therapy, Recreational Therapy, Art Therapy, Music Therapy, Dance or Movement Therapy, Rolfing, and Child or Family Therapy. Art, Music, and Dance therapies are sometimes classified as Expressive Therapies. These adjunctive therapies are often offered in residential settings such as hospitals, nursing homes, group homes, or in programs which involve a several-day-a-week time commitment.

Occupational Therapy (OT) offers a range of services from arts and crafts to job skills. In hospitals or residential settings there may be a fully equipped OT room where workers help people with individualized projects. With patients who are severely emotionally disturbed or physically ill, the first goal of OT may be to interest them in a simple project such as gluing mosaic tile or making enamel ashtrays. People who are functioning at a higher level are generally involved in projects requiring more skill and the following of complex directions. Recreational therapists may help to plan structured games and activities for groups in and out of the hospital. These may be helpful in getting people to be active or may help them deal with issues such as competition, teamwork, or cooperation. The activities might range from playing volleyball on the hospital grounds to organizing a trip to a local beach. Recreational therapists may be helping patients get in touch with resources they can use when they leave a hospital setting or helping to keep them active while in the hospital.

EXPRESSIVE THERAPIES

The Expressive Therapies usually take place in groups, but some therapists use these techniques in individual therapy or incorporate various techniques into their work. If a specific technique appeals to you, it can probably be useful, since it would help you to explore your problems from a different viewpoint.

Art Therapy uses various kinds of art materials to help people experience their feelings or express things they may find difficult to say in words. Therapists may suggest individual projects for clients or may have group members participate together in structured and unstructured exercises. Dance and Music Therapy use different kinds of music and movements to help people express themselves.

Expressive Therapy groups can help you to experience yourself in a totally new way. If you feel uncomfortable participating in something labeled art or dance, you may find yourself saying, "I can't draw (sing, dance, paint, act, etc.)." You need not be embarrassed by your talents (or lack of them). Groups like these help you to use materials or your body to express how *you* feel, not to compete with some abstract standard of art or performance. It can also be helpful if you push yourself to try something which seems difficult to you; but never let yourself get forced into something which makes you feel awkward, embarrassed, or humiliated. You always have the right to say no.

ROLFING

Rolfing was invented by Dr. Ida Rolf and is a technique for restructuring the body so as to bring its major segments (head, shoulders, thorax, pelvis, and legs) toward a vertical alignment. The average person, through bad posture, chronic tension, or accident, has let her body weight slip out of the vertical axis—head slumped forward, shoulders hunched, or buttocks carried up and back. In consequence, the body locks up, and joints lose their freedom, circulation is restricted, and the person may live with constant pain and fatigue. Through a series of ten hour-long sessions, manual pressure is carefully applied to realign muscles and connective tissues. The process is surprisingly painful, physically, and the client often experiences emotional pain as well, when the rolfer works on areas that are particularly tense or rigid.

Rolfers claim that, as a result of feeling more self-confident after rolfing, a client will feel better, have more energy, look taller, not be constantly tense, and be better able to deal with emotional stress. One problem is that the body continues to be subjected to destructive forces. Therefore, rolfing must be an ongoing process. Since this is strictly a physical technique, it can be painful. The rolfer may or may not have experience with psychological therapy or social issues; so, if you choose to be rolfed, be sure to interview the therapist carefully.

CHILD OR FAMILY THERAPY

Child Therapy or Family Therapy are obviously used mainly when children are involved. When children have problems at school, have overwhelming fears or anxieties, have learning problems for which there is no apparent perceptual basis, or other emotional problems, therapy may be recommended. Often children are treated at a child guidance clinic or a family service agency, or they may be seen by a private therapist who specializes in children. With very young children, it may be difficult or impossible to use the kinds of verbal therapy that work with adults. Instead, therapy often utilizes play materials such as dolls, clay, or paints, allowing the child to work through feelings symbolically. Children may do very well in groups using psychodrama or other movement techniques.

Usually, when a child is in therapy, family members are expected to be in therapy also. The parents may be asked to have regular appointments, or the whole family may come for treatment. This may be done with several therapists, and family members may be seen separately and then together in various combinations. Some agencies do *network therapy* in which they ask not only immediate family members to participate but also other relatives and friends. You have a right to know what kind of therapy a therapist is considering, and why. You also have some say in what you wish to participate in. The focus in Family Therapy is usually on the dynamics of the family and on ways to change the interactions or alliances between family members, so that relationships can improve. The therapist(s) may give some specific advice, but should not lecture the family or try to make one family member feel guilty about what s/he has been doing.

Alternatives to Therapy

No matter what form therapy takes—analytic, non-directive, experiential, or directive, individual, or group— there is still a common denominator: you are going to a professional whom you have paid to be there and concentrating on working out your problems. There are many reasons why you might decide against psychotherapy. Perhaps politically you are against psychotherapy and "professionalism"; perhaps you feel you would like to solve your problems yourself rather than rely on someone else's expertise. Or maybe you resent the idea of a relationship which involves a certain amount of dependence on someone who is neither a friend, lover, nor family member. The stigma of seeing a "shrink" may be too great, or you may feel your particular problems don't belong in a therapist's office.

Many people are reluctant to enter therapy for these or other personal reasons. If you think you might need to be in therapy but balk at the idea, one option you have is to interview one or two therapists and contract to meet with one for a very limited time (perhaps four sessions). You might then be better able to judge whether or not therapy is right for you. If, on the other hand, you already know you don't want therapy, there are alternatives to consider.

Some alternatives to therapy, such as consciousness-raising groups or some support groups, have been designed by women for women; others, like Mental Patients Liberation Front groups, are for women and men who have shared the experience of hospitalization. Still others, like Arica or encounter groups, are part of a general humanistic, personal-growth movement. We urge you to consider these alternatives carefully. Many can be useful both as alternatives or adjuncts to therapy. Choose on the basis of what will meet your needs right now, rather than on the claims of advertising or of enthusiastic supporters of a particular group.

ENCOUNTER GROUPS

Encounter groups became popular in the late 1960s with workshops run by Fritz Perls (founder of Gestalt therapy) at Esalen Institute in Big Sur, California. Esalen was the first of the "personal growth" resorts to be organized and promoted as a big-business approach to therapy. Today such organizations are found all over the country, some with permanent headquarters and membership, others just quickly organized weekends at various motels or camps. The essence of these groups is to offer a sort of supermarket of services, with group leaders who have various styles and credentials.

Encounter groups have a persistent anti-intellectual strain which resists theory, order, or systematization. Psychotherapy systems, methods, and training are considered irrelevant to people's basic needs for deeply-experienced relationships with others. At their best, encounter groups offer warmth and closeness; at their worst, a mish-mash of semi-helpful, quasi-religious mumbo jumbo.

A "Meaningful Experience"

Some encounter group leaders have been trained in one of the many psychotherapy systems and then have moved into the encounter methodology; most, however, have gone through the encounter group experience themselves and then become group leaders—and thus have no other frame of reference. The group is meant to provide an intense emotional experience through structured and unstructured encounters with other people. The group not only gives permission to feel; it demands openness, bluntness, and expression of any sort that is free from social prohibitions. This can involve confrontation, massage, hugging, dancing, nudity, screaming, arm-wrestling—anything that encourages uninhibited interaction among group members. This short-term intimacy (the group lasts anywhere from a few hours to several weeks) is intended to be a therapeutic experience and to provide the antidote to isolation and unhappiness. Other goals of the encounter experience are learning to communicate, overcoming shyness, breaking through defenses, and getting feedback about one's patterns of relating.

Evaluation

People do not enter encounter groups as clients seeking help with their emotional problems, but as individuals who want more meaning and spontaneity in their lives. Unfortunately, there is little or no screening of participants by group leaders, no follow-up after the group is disbanded, and group leaders take no responsibility for what happens to participants. Although many people feel they benefit from these groups, others criticize the inability of either the leaders or group members to look critically at what they do. Group members who question the group or criticize the leader are likely to be ostracized. There is also evidence that encounter groups can be harmful to those seeking emotional stability. A study by Yalom and Lieberman[1] found that 16 of 130 Stanford University students who completed encounter groups could be considered "casualties," which means they found some evidence of "serious psychological harm" caused by their participation in the group. This study is distressing because it showed that group leaders were less aware of which members were hurt than were other group members.

Encounter groups have been satisfying for some people who want an interesting experience that might promote emotional growth and that allows them to try out a "different self." However, people who have serious and specific problems to work on are apt to be frustrated in such a group; the rest of the group may be concerned primarily with "feeling joy" and may not want to focus on sadness or expend energy on difficult, long-term emotional problems.

If you are considering joining an encounter group, evaluate the leader and her/his values carefully beforehand. The feelings and opinions of the group leader, as well as those of the co-participants, are apt to be pressed very strongly on you. "Touchy-feely" games are often valued as liberating, and your refusal or reluctance to participate in them may bring forth accusations of being uptight or in need of special help. The games may be a helpful way to get in touch with yourself, or they may simply be a way for someone else to get in touch with your body. You should have the final say about what you take part in, and the atmosphere should be free enough to allow you to make that decision and not make you feel guilty at being "un-liberated." At the same time, no one should go to an en-counter group with the expectation that they will be al-lowed to be a voyeur. If the avowed goal is to learn more about yourself, you should expect to do some sharing.

ARICA

Arica is a system of spiritual development and enlighten-ment developed in 1965 by Oscar Ichazo, a Bolivian. In 1971 an Arica Training Institute was founded in New York City and has since offered training programs nation-wide.

There are many levels of Arica training, some of which can be completed without a trained guide or training manuals. Other intensive training sessions last from three weeks to forty days and are conducted by special trainers. People spend twelve hours a day together, practicing a mixture of yoga exercises, psychodrama, and Gestalt exer-cises, meditation, and self-criticism. They abstain from alcohol, tobacco, and other tension-releasing substances. They engage in intense discussion with one another, re-vealing many intimate facts about their lives.

Evaluation

Arica training is typical of the personal growth/spiritual kinds of encounter experiences that are offered today under many different names. You may enjoy an experi-ence like this, and you may find it changes your life; but it is definitely not a substitute for psychotherapy. If, for example, you are experiencing difficulties in relating to others or feel unhappy about areas of your life such as work or studies, it is unlikely that an experience such as Arica would help and likely that it would intensify some feelings of distress since you will be pushed into intense relationships that may be too hard to handle.

EST

"est" is an acronym for Erhard Seminars Training, a creation of Werner Erhard. Erhard, who changed his name from Jack Rosenberg after separating from his wife and children in 1960, developed "est" after experiencing a transformation in his own life. Once he had experienced what he perceived as the perfection of life, he incorporated "est" so that he could share his experience with others. Erhard had sampled various disciplines such as yoga, Scientology, Gestalt, encounter groups, and many others, and has used all of them to create a standard training session called "est."

The training, which lasts sixty hours (usually over two weekends), takes place in a large room—a hotel ballroom or conference room. Approximately 250 people gather to be lectured to by "est" staff members on the "est" philosophy. Bathroom privileges and eating breaks are severely restricted, participants sit on hard chairs, and are told to refrain from talking with one another or leaving their seats. Three things happen during the training: (1) a presentation that encourages participants to examine their own belief systems; (2) training in meditation, during which participants are instructed to "experience their own experience"; and (3) group communication, in which participants are called on to ask questions or share their insights about the training.

There is one simple message to "est": you are the cause of your own experience and responsible for your own life. If you get this message, then in the "est" parlance, you have "gotten it." If this seems confusing, it is because there is nothing more to "est" than that message; and yet

Erhard has convinced thousands of people to spend $300 each for receiving it.

Evaluation

"est" is very successful—a nine-million-dollar business in 1975, and growing every year. One reason for the financial success, besides the high price, is the use of volunteers (people who have gone through the "est" experience and "gotten it") who become trainers. "est" has its casualties— not only those who don't "get it," but some who develop psychotic symptoms after "est" training.[2] But despite the scoffs of the skeptics (mostly psychotherapists), "est" is generally praised by those who go through the experience. Erhard's success probably stems from his insight into how to break down defenses. Resistance is lowered by the tedium, the haranguing of the trainer, and deprivation of ordinary tension release (smoking, drinking, drug use, eating, or just going to the bathroom). The size of the group also helps build tension and leads a person to dissolve her individuality and to merge with the others.

The result is a state of receptivity, openness, and weakened discrimination. The trainer fills the gap with the "est" philosophy: "Take responsibility for yourself and you can be anything you want to be." This explains the enthusiasm and genuine praise the participants express for such pronouncements as, "Well, turkeys, you just paid out $300 for zip. All I've told you is that what is, is, and what isn't, isn't." It also explains the worshipful attitude of trainers and converts toward Erhard, whom they regard as little less than God. The ethics of such an approach are not clear and must be left up to each individual to evaluate for herself.

CO-COUNSELING OR RE-EVALUATION COUNSELING

Co-counseling is a form of peer counseling that works on an exchange basis. Two women agree to meet regularly and co-counsel each other, each taking half the time to be counselor and half to be client; or each woman may use counseling time as she needs it and pay it back when she can. In order to learn to do this effectively, they attend co-counseling groups where they discuss and practice the co-counseling ideas and skills. Participants pay a small fee for attending groups.

According to its originator Harvey Jackins, the theory behind co-counseling is that the pain people experience is due to rigid patterns of suppressing grief or pain at the time of its occurrence and storing up the experience. Jackins observed that infants and young children show a variety of reactions following a painful event, be it emotional or physical, and theorized that they were naturally and spontaneously discharging the pain. When they learn to suppress these reactions, theoretically they store up the pain. The process of co-counseling helps the client discharge the painful emotion through tears, laughter, shaking, trembling, talking, or whatever is necessary.

The counseling role in co-counseling is a fairly passive one; the counselor encourages the client by listening attentively, asking occasional questions, or possibly repeating something the client says. The governing attitude of the counselors is "don't interfere." Emotional expression of clients should come spontaneously and not be suggested or prompted by the counselor. The client decides what to work on, and the experience is essentially self-directed.

Because co-counseling involves an emotional exchange which heightens the feelings both people may have about each other, there are some specific guidelines about socializing. The co-counseling manual (the *Blue Pages*) specifies that people co-counseling each other refrain from any other relationship with each other. Friends or lovers who enter co-counseling may do so together, however, or they may join different groups; the proscription of close friendship or sex is only directed at people who meet in co-counseling.

Evaluation

Traditional therapists have criticized co-counseling because many feel that a counselor or therapist needs special skills (such as the ability to explore emotional problems in depth) which are not learned in the co-counseling process. Some therapists also feel that the exchange of counselor/client roles is not really possible because the client needs someone in the permanent role of therapist. Other criticisms from less traditional quarters are similar. For example, that the client may not be able to make an exchange of services or may not want to. She may feel that she needs a longer period of time only for herself and is not able to even listen to another person's problems. Another criticism is that co-counseling is too simplistic, that emotional discharge is dramatic but does not have any long-term effects.

The positive aspects of co-counseling are that it is egalitarian and that it attempts to build a community of women (and men) who can be available to one another. Some of the groups in which co-counseling skills are learned are focused on specific issues, such as single parenthood or divorce, so that participants will begin with some shared experience. There is a definite attempt on the part of co-counselors to build a community, or network, of people around the country who make themselves available to each other and who share the co-counseling philosophy.

ASSERTIVENESS TRAINING

Although Assertiveness Training is a technique which can be used to help anyone who has trouble being assertive, it has become more and more popular with women in recent years because of their efforts to move out of the home and the passive "feminine" role. Many Assertiveness Training groups have been organized in women's centers and are regarded as an important part of the

Women's Movement. Group leaders see a connection between the stereotyped roles that women have been conditioned to play in our society and the need for Assertiveness Training to enable women to break out of these stereotypes. Some groups not affiliated with the Women's Movement are more technique-oriented and do not deal with the specific needs of women. These groups, especially if run by a man, may end up not only not helping a woman overcome her non-assertiveness, but making her feel guilty for not being assertive.

What Is "Assertiveness"?

The non-assertive person, because of high levels of anxiety and guilt about her feelings, tends to bottle up emotions. As a result, this person may have trouble asking for her needs to be met, socializing comfortably with other people, speaking up in a discussion, expressing feelings to friends, dealing with tradespeople, or accepting a compliment from someone without refuting or demeaning it. Non-assertive people are often victimized by others because they cannot say "no" to unreasonable requests and are unable to verbally protect themselves when someone nags or criticizes them unfairly. Non-assertive people are often depressed, have a poor self-image, and see themselves as being at the mercy of the world around them.

Assertiveness Training combines a humanistic philosophy of therapy with a behavioral approach. The group member learns, through rehearsing behaviors in the group, to recognize herself as an important person who is entitled to thoughts, emotions, and feelings which need not be sacrificed or negotiated away in a relationship with someone else, regardless of whether or not the relationship is an intimate or a superficial one. Modesty is exchanged for acknowledging one's own positive attributes and accepting the compliments and praise given by others. Participants learn that if they want people to know what they are thinking or feeling, they have the responsibility to communicate it and not assume that it will be known intuitively.

Evaluation

Assertiveness is often confused with aggressiveness. The difference is that the aggressive person stands up for her rights in such a way that the rights of others are violated. The purpose of aggressive behavior is to dominate, humiliate, or put the other person down in order to make the aggressor feel good about herself because the other person feels bad. The purpose of assertiveness is to enjoy self-respect while respecting others, and to communicate feelings and thoughts honestly.

We recommend Assertiveness Training when these principles are followed. It can be an alternative or an adjunct to psychotherapy. Women learning from each other to respect themselves is the essence of a positive therapeutic experience for women, providing the values promoted in the group are non-exploitative and healthy ones.

CONSCIOUSNESS-RAISING GROUPS (C-R)

Consciousness-Raising groups became popular in the late 1960s and early 1970s, at a time when the impact of the Women's Movement had extended beyond those who were politically radical and was reaching greater numbers of American women. C-R groups still exist today, but they are less common than "support" groups. Although C-R groups are still being organized in the cities, they are more likely to be found now in suburban areas.

How Does C-R Work?

Therapy can't be separate from raising a woman's consciousness about her connections to other women, her oppression and her need to be a strong, self-actualized human being.

C-R groups are usually small, consisting of six to twelve women, and almost always leaderless. The purpose of the group is to share personal experiences and feelings so that each woman discovers that what she may have thought was a personal dilemma is really a social predicament that is shared by many women. Members take turns talking and listening, sharing and analyzing, and drawing conclusions. The process is one of transforming the hidden, individual fears of women into a shared awareness of their meaning as social problems. Because of the sharing of each other's experiences, members often discover options for personal growth and change that they never knew existed. Women often end up feeling a commitment to the struggle against oppression in their own lives and the lives of all women.

The initial purpose of C-R groups was to raise the consciousness of members of the oppression of women and how it affects them personally. It was necessary to use a structured group because women, unlike other oppressed groups, are not a ghettoized minority and often did not have the opportunity to recognize the similar ways in which all women were oppressed. Either a woman felt that she was the only one who was suffering a particular problem, or she felt that she was not oppressed and that other women were inferior or unable to assert themselves. Only in the intimate atmosphere of C-R could many women learn to see themselves as part of a larger group of women.

What I got out of my women's group was just sharing opinions, gaining knowledge that other people suffer from the same problems, meeting new people, and getting out of the house!

How to Find a C-R Group

Women looking for C-R groups can often find meetings at a local women's organization (National Organization for Women, League of Women Voters, a women's center, or

school) which organize groups and then leave them to
operate on their own. In the absence of such organizations,
many women decide to start groups on their own. Claudia
Dreifus offers some ideas for starting groups without organizational help in her book *Woman's Fate.*[3]

Find five to twelve members, either by talking to women
friends and neighbors, posting signs where women con-
gregate to do their work (e.g., company cafeteria, day-care
centers, supermarkets), hand out leaflets, or put an ad in
the local newspaper. Do not invite men to become members—their presence inevitably inhibits women from
speaking freely and openly. The best place to meet is in
women's homes, taking turns from week to week, if possible. Weekly meetings are best, and regular attendance is
important to insure continuity and a sense of trust.

Members should take turns being in charge of the meeting. If no one has experience doing this, groups sometimes
hire a Feminist therapist to work with them for a few
sessions to help get things started. Begin sessions by allowing everyone a turn to speak for five or ten minutes and
follow that with questions and answers, debate, and then
analysis of what has been discussed. Many groups find it
helpful at first to decide on specific topics for each meeting, such as marriage, sex roles, children, work, or sexuality.

Evaluation

Some problems that crop up are the domination of the
group by one member or a few members, negative feelings
like conflict or competition not being dealt with, or dwell-
ing on relationships with men. These problems can be
overcome if they are confronted and dealt with honestly.
Group members should always keep in mind that C-R is
not meant to be therapy; its purpose is essentially political.
Women have been conditioned to believe that they can't
get along with each other, but this conditioning can be
overcome.

Like Assertiveness Training, Consciousness-Raising can be both an alternative and an adjunct to therapy. The unique experience of learning how other women share problems you thought you alone were experiencing has truly been the essence of the Women's Movement for many of us.

SUPPORT GROUPS

Support group is a loose term used to describe a small group of women meeting together to deal with a specific issue. Sometimes these are informal groups; others are organized by an agency or umbrella group. They may be characterized as self-help groups because they usually consist of women who have common experience of a particular problem and who get together to work on that problem for themselves and others, with or without the support of professionals.

One example of a support group in the Boston area is an organization called COPE (Coping with the Overall Pregnancy/Parenting Experience). COPE helps organize small groups of women (and, more recently, groups of men) who discuss issues of parenting. These groups have a leader who takes responsibility for organizing the groups, checking on absent members, and making sure that each member gets a chance to talk. Since the leader has also been through the experience of being a mother, she may be able to share helpful ways of dealing with problems. She does not have the responsibility of being a therapist; she is simply taking organizational and administrative responsibility for the group.

Another support group model is one that has been used by ex-mental patients around the country. A weekly meeting is held which is open to all ex-patients in the community who wish to attend and get support for such issues as avoiding hospitalization, dealing with the social stigma of prior hospitalization, getting back into the community, or making friends. These groups often do not have a leader, but rely on old members helping new members become part of the group and feel welcome.

Women often use the support group model in a variety of ways to increase their contact with other women and to establish a support network of friends and colleagues in the community. Many women feel that they do not need the kind of discussion that a consciousness-raising group might offer, but that they do need to talk and gain support from other women who might be working in their field or pursuing similar interests. Many women experience stress that is impossible to deal with alone but becomes manageable when they are sustained by the friendship and concern of others.

Evaluation

Other topics for support groups are: health care (short-term, self-help groups are often formed at women's health centers to enable women to learn about their bodies and how to do vaginal self-examination), sex education, political study, unemployment and the return to work, drug abuse, alcoholism, and divorce and separation. All of these are also areas in which professionally-organized counseling help may be available, and it is up to each woman to decide if she wants to go to a support group or a professional agency. The attitudes and values imparted by the different types of groups may themselves be very different. For example, many hospitals and out-patient mental health facilities have groups for ex-patients which are controlled by professional staff who will decide whether or not a particular person needs to be rehospitalized. Ex-patient groups controlled by the patients are more interested in helping people stay out of hospitals. Groups which are entirely patient-run may therefore have a more positive philosophy.

Many of the larger self-help support groups, such as Mental Patients Liberation, came into existence in order to fill a gap in the care that was offered professionally. We feel that professionals often sabotage the self-help movement by criticizing it as amateurish. Certain values are lost, however, when groups are professionally-run, and clients once again become dependent on someone else for a service. Self-help support groups encourage women to take responsibility for themselves and learn how to develop their own resources.

I was in a group of women of various ages and with various problems. Each worked on sharing (or airing) her own problems under conditions of mutual support, sometimes finding a partial answer even in the knowledge that one is not alone in having that problem or hang-up.

NOTES

1. Irvin Yalom and Morton Lieberman, "A Study of Encounter Group Casualties," *Progress in Group and Family Therapy,* Clifford Sager and Helen Singer Kaplan, eds. (New York: 1972), p. 223.

2. Leonard L. Glass, M.D., Michael A. Kirsch, M.D., and Frederick N. Parris, M.D., "Psychiatric Disturbances Associated with Erhard Seminars Training: I. A Report of Cases," *The American Journal of Psychiatry* 134:3, March 1977, pp. 245–7.

3. Claudia Dreifus, *Woman's Fate.*

Chapter 9

Credentials and Titles

Psychotherapists come from many different backgrounds. Psychology, social work, and medicine are the three major areas, but counseling, the ministry, nursing, teaching, and other widely varying occupations also produce psychotherapists. You will probably encounter a number of different titles and credentials when searching for a therapist. Remember that learning what a therapist's credentials are is just a starting point, not the sole criterion for choice. There are a number of reasons why the therapist's background may be important to you, but we urge you to consider much more than credentials in making this important decision.

No particular credentials are necessarily the "best." Credentials do no more than allow you to make some generalizations about what to expect of a particular therapist. You must also take into consideration how experienced the therapist is, what techniques s/he uses, what her/his values are concerning women's roles, and, most important, whether or not you feel comfortable working with her/him.

There are a few titles which have a specific and generally agreed-upon meaning; they usually refer to persons with certain academic and clinical training. Many states have laws controlling the use of certain titles, but these laws vary substantially from state to state. For example, in all states a psychiatrist must be an M.D., but there may be no requirements that s/he have specialized training in mental health. Although unlikely, it is therefore possible for a psychiatrist to hang out her/his shingle without ever having taken a single class in therapy or seen a single client. In many states the title psychologist is controlled by law and can be used only by a person who has a Ph.D. and who has received clinical training and passed an examination. However, in other states, the title psychologist is not controlled and may be used by anyone with or without training, degrees, or expertise.

Some of the other titles used by therapists are not only not legally controlled but are vague in meaning. Therapist, psychotherapist, and counselor are all terms which do not have any specific or agreed-upon meaning. They may be used interchangeably, or the therapist may have a very specific rationale as to why s/he uses a particular title. Some titles, such as psychiatric nurse, tell you something about the person's background, that is, that s/he has a degree in nursing and some specialization and/or interest in psychiatry; but this does not say anything about what additional training s/he may have. Others, such as Feminist therapist, indicate a political stance but reveal nothing about educational or professional credentials. Professional titles like psychologist or psychiatrist say something about the educational level attained by the person but nothing about their political or philosophical orientation, and possibly nothing about their training as a therapist.

For convenience, we have grouped the titles in the following way:

Medical Titles—Family Doctor, Psychiatrist, Psychiatric Nurse, Psychoanalyst;

Non-Medical Titles: Specific—Social Worker, Psychologist, Counselor (Guidance, Marriage, Pastoral), Student Therapist;

Non-Medical Titles: Non-Specific—Psychotherapist, Sex Therapist, Mental Health Worker, Feminist Therapist.

Medical Titles

FAMILY DOCTOR

The family doctor is not a psychotherapist, but we include this title here because many people turn first to their family doctor as someone they trust and whom they expect to have some expertise in dealing with emotional problems. When family or sexual problems are involved, people have often been urged to consult their family physician. Some doctors recognize this role and are prepared to help direct patients to the appropriate resources; others are extremely skeptical of psychiatry ("It's not *real* medicine") or any mental health services. They may insist that the patient does not have a problem and that she should concentrate on "feeling better" or, what is possibly worse, they may treat the patient with tranquilizers, stimulants, or other mood-altering drugs.

Doctors are bombarded with advertising in medical journals urging them to prescribe tranquilizers or mood-altering drugs for their patients and often implying that such drugs are the only treatment necessary. When it comes to other problems, which are both psychological and physiological, the doctor may end up treating only one part of the problem. For example, some women going through menopause have been treated solely with drugs, while the psychological issues confronting them were ignored. In addition, they have been offered no choice in how to treat the physical discomforts they may experience; it has been assumed that they must take drugs.

Other women have been given tranquilizers to treat physical symptoms and have ended up with increased emotional problems. For example, one woman reports, "I have taken 'tranqs,' of course, prescribed by the good old family doctor for heart palpitations and colitis. They absolutely weren't helpful. One prescription plunged me into the actual depression which finally got me to go to my therapist. I feel that the medication provided the doctor with the feeling that he'd *done* something. He never has followed up on the medication to see if it helped or if I needed something else."

The greatest drawback of physicians is that they have had little or no exposure to psychiatry, psychological theories of development, or even to ordinary interactions between people as a result of the overwhelming demands of what has become the increasingly technical study of medicine. The model for treating physical illness (diagnosis, treatment, and cure) is awkward and unsuited to most psychological problems; and furthermore, the medical model of delegating treatment to inferiors (nurses and aides who have less power and authority) by writing "orders" (directions left by doctors for specific medical treatment such as drugs or physical therapy), is completely unsuited to treating psychological problems.

If you do turn to a doctor for help, you should be able to expect a thorough physical exam to help rule out any organic basis for your problems. If the doctor is willing to make a referral, it will most often be to someone else in the medical field, probably a psychiatrist. You need to be aware that there are other resources that your doctor might not know about. Do not accept a prescription for psychotropic drugs (tranquilizers, mood elevators, energizers, "something for your nerves") in lieu of a thorough exploration of your needs. Such drugs should be taken only in conjunction with psychotherapy and then only with a full explanation of their action and possible side effects.

PSYCHIATRIST

Contrary to popular opinion, the title psychiatrist does not necessarily guarantee good mental health care. The use of this title is legally limited to medical doctors in all states but says nothing about their further training beyond M.D. Any physician who has a valid M.D. license can decide at any time to practice psychiatry—with or without further training. Most doctors interested in psychiatry, however, do undergo a three-year residency after completing an internship, but it can vary from residency in a large state hospital setting where s/he participates in minimal classes and is in charge of hundreds of patients, to residency in a smaller, more prestigious training hospital where s/he will attend extensive classes and have closely supervised therapy experiences. Psychiatrists can be certified by taking the American Board of Psychiatry and Neurology exam, but less than half of the psychiatrists practicing in the United States have taken these exams. They may instead state that they are *board-eligible,* meaning that they have completed all the requirements except the exam. Even when they are board-certified, their overall skills in psychotherapy have not been tested—just such areas as diagnosis, classification of symptoms, and use of medication.

Psychiatrists, like any therapists, are to be found in many settings and have varying degrees of skill. Many psychiatrists have a private practice but are also affiliated with a hospital or mental health clinic, and their fees may differ from one location to another. Fees of psychiatrists in private practice are generally higher than those of other therapists.

Psychiatrists are the only mental health professionals

permitted to prescribe medication or use shock treatment (ECT), and they have the greatest accessibility to hospitalization for patients. This is not necessarily an advantage, since they often use these treatments as the only form of therapy, rather than as adjuncts to psychotherapy. Psychiatrists used to be split between those who followed psychoanalytic methods and those who relied heavily on somatic (physical) treatments. This split was more heavily emphasized in the 1950s than is now the case, as a recent survey in 1975 shows. Now the homogenization of treatment is more evident, with almost all psychiatrists prescribing drugs for their own patients and routinely prescribing drugs for patients treated by other mental health professionals.[1]

Foreign medical school graduates may be employed as ward physicians in a mental hospital (where they can work before taking the American licensing exams for physicians). This often confuses patients and families who may think they are consulting a psychiatrist, since these doctors are responsible for prescribing psychotropic drugs. Foreign medical school graduates cannot call themselves psychiatrists, however, since they are not yet licensed. They may be adequate physicians; but since their grasp of the English language is often poor, they may not understand what a patient is saying.

PSYCHIATRIC NURSE

The title psychiatric nurse refers to a nurse who specializes in the field of mental health. S/he has graduated from a nursing program, either as a practical nurse (L.P.N.) or a registered nurse (R.N.). All nurses receive theoretical and practical training in psychiatric nursing, usually several months of working on a psychiatric in-patient unit. Although there is no special license or certification for psychiatric nurses, a number of schools now offer graduate training leading to a Master of Science degree or Ph.D.

in psychiatric nursing. This may include courses in psychotherapy and supervised therapy experience. Some state nursing associations award a certificate in psychiatric nursing to nurses completing this type of program.

Because of their training in the medical model, which emphasizes the doctor as the primary decision maker and the nurse as the person designated to follow the doctor's treatment plan, few nurses go into private practice as psychotherapists. Often nurses with higher degrees are channeled into administrative or supervisory positions within institutions and not encouraged to seek independent clinical settings. However, a growing number are responsible for psychiatric care in in-patient units, in follow-up out-patient clinics, in nursing homes, and in health-related agency settings.

PSYCHOANALYST

The term psychoanalyst is not controlled by law and can theoretically be used by anyone. For the most part, it refers to someone who has undergone specialized training at a psychoanalytic institute identified with one of the major schools of therapy, usually Freudian or neo-Freudian in approach. Almost all of the members of these institutes are medical doctors; a few people from other professions are admitted, especially to programs in child analysis, and are referred to as *lay analysts.*

Psychoanalysts who attend analytic training institutes have usually completed medical school, an internship, probably a psychiatric residency of three years, and are undergoing or have undergone their own personal analysis. This means that they have invested considerable time, money and energy to get where they are and therefore are apt to be set in a particular way of working, usually with a focus on early childhood events and the interpretation of the unconscious. They often feel justified in charging high fees for their work (as much as $50 to $100 per fifty-minute hour). Therefore, if you decide to see an analyst, you should be sure that this is the method and theoretical approach you want.

Non-Medical Titles: Specific

SOCIAL WORKER

In some states this title is controlled by law and indicates that the person has a Master's Degree in Social Work from an accredited graduate program and has taken a licensing examination. Many people with this title were licensed or certified under "grandfather clauses," meaning that they were practicing social work when these laws went into effect. There are also B.A. programs in social work, and in some places the title social worker has been used to refer to anyone doing work in social agencies, ranging from welfare case administrator to working with abused children. Other people working for state or local agencies may be exempt from licensing requirements and may use the title social worker even though they do not have a specific degree.

Usually the title social worker refers to someone who has completed a two-year graduate program concentrating on casework, group work or community organization. Social workers study both interpersonal dynamics and the social forces that affect people and also do field work placements to practice their skills. Social work education has always emphasized how societal pressures affect people's lives, particularly pressures such as poverty and racial prejudice. Social workers are likely to have worked in a variety of settings and with many different classes of people.

Social work was for many years considered a woman's profession, despite the fact that many men also went into the field. However, as in many service professions, women tended to do the direct service, while men moved into the administrative positions. Even though social workers often confronted issues of classism and racism in their work with clients, it is only recently that the social work literature has begun to reflect the growing concern of women within the profession for how these very issues affect their own status and lives. Social workers have always regarded themselves as models for their clients, and women social workers now want to be able to be strong female models for their women clients.

A social worker (or intake worker) may be your first contact in many family-service or child-guidance agencies. They are also the people who usually do the direct service in these agencies. There are many social workers in private practice doing individual, group, or family therapy, as well.

PSYCHOLOGIST

The meaning of the title psychologist varies from state to state, so you should check with the state psychological association to determine what the requirements for its use are in your particular state. Where psychologists are certified or licensed, this usually indicates that they are required to have a Ph.D. or Ed.D. in psychology, educational psychology, counseling, or school psychology from an accredited school. Additionally, state licensing boards may require passing a written examination and undergoing a certain amount of supervised experience in clinical psychology. Under "grandfather clauses," those persons who do not meet these requirements, but had already been practicing as psychologists when the law went into effect, or those persons working in a state, county, or municipal agency, may be covered by the law and eligible for licensing. All of these requirements are confusing, and we mention them only to point out that the use of this particular title doesn't tell you much. In states where its use is controlled by law, it often means the practitioner can receive third-party payments from insurance companies. In other states it may mean the practitioner has an M.A. degree in any of several fields.

Just as licensing requirements vary from state to state, so, too, do training programs vary from school to school. Many psychologists are trained to teach and do research rather than practice psychotherapy. Some clinical psychology programs, although offering supervised practice during an internship (sometimes called a practicum or placement), still emphasize the use of various diagnostic tests rather than psychotherapy skills.* Psychologists are legally free to work in all areas of the field, even though the American Psychological Association's code of ethics says they can function only in their field of competence. Psychologists who are interested in pursuing psychotherapy as a major interest often enroll in a training institute or program that is identified with one of the major approaches to therapy. Most of these programs offer some kind of certification, but no degree. A certificate of this sort usually means that the psychologist identifies with the particular school of therapy and will use it in practice.

Some clinical psychologists are certified by the American Board of Examiners in Professional Psychology, which examines therapeutic skills. Few psychologists take the examination, though, because it requires the applicant to present verbatim descriptions of her/his therapy sessions and recommend a therapeutic plan for a client seen during the examination.

Any person with a Ph.D. may be addressed as "doctor." For example, Jane Smith, Ph.D. is also Dr. Jane Smith. Therefore, if you are referred to a therapist with the title of doctor, you cannot assume s/he is a physician.

---

*Some psychologists may rely heavily on various testing procedures. Many psychological tests are highly speculative and have been criticized for their biases. This is especially true of I.Q. tests and various interpretive tests used to track children in schools.

COUNSELOR

Though the title counselor is not controlled by law in most states and may be used by anyone, with or without a degree, it generally indicates someone who has a Master of Arts degree in Educational Counseling and has spent one or two years in an accredited graduate program. Some people use the title to indicate that they practice counseling rather than therapy, counseling being presumed to be more superficial, dealing with present-oriented, day-to-day problems of living, while therapy presumably deals with more crippling psychoneurotic or psychotic problems. However, these distinctions are by no means universal. The title counselor is also used by the following, more specific groups:

VOCATIONAL COUNSELOR—CAREER COUNSELOR. A vocational counselor specializes in work-related issues, such as unemployment, job preference, or educational and training needs. In many bureaucratic agencies, the counselor may have little or no training for the job and no special skills; it is often just an administrative title. The vocational counselor is also in charge of programs for retraining the physically or emotionally handicapped person, for providing funds to such people, and for coordinating the services to each person from a number of different agencies.

There are a number of private agencies specializing in vocational or career counseling for women who are trying to re-enter the work force. They may offer personal counseling, support groups for the unemployed, assertiveness training, interviewing skills, résumé writing, or actual job referrals. Anyone visiting such an agency should check on what services are actually offered and what fees are charged. Beware of agencies that make the same recommendations to every client, no matter what her interests.

If an agency implies that you will get a job, find out what the guarantees are. A high fee is no guarantee of the quality of service offered. Many community colleges now offer special vocational programs for women returning to work and may offer more extensive services for less money. Elaborate (and expensive) vocational testing is unnecessary and undesirable unless you are interested in a specific or highly technical field.

GUIDANCE COUNSELOR. Guidance counselors usually have a Master's degree in Education and may also be certified to teach school. They usually work in high schools or community colleges and help students with educational and vocational choices. They may give extensive tests to students or simply provide brief counseling. Depending on the size of the school, they may have a personal knowledge of the student or they may have access only to a file folder containing the student's test scores.

Guidance counselors do not usually give personal counseling to students or families, but in some schools they may be the first person to make contact with the families of children who are not doing well for a variety of reasons. They may make recommendations or referrals for psychotherapy to other agencies in the community; but since the guidance counselor has rarely had much training in psychotherapy, it is wise to have other referral sources as well. Because of the recent passage of laws concerning special-needs children, some schools may have guidance counselors who are better attuned to the needs of these children and to the facilities available for both parents and children.

MARRIAGE COUNSELOR, FAMILY COUNSELOR, COUPLES COUNSELOR. Any of these titles may be used by a person who specializes in working with couples or families. There is an American Association of Marriage Counselors which sets some minimum standards for membership; its membership includes people from various backgrounds, such as sociologists, social workers, or physicians. Not everyone using the title marriage counselor belongs to this association, however. Some training institutes award certificates in marriage or family counseling. Other therapists, who don't specifically identify themselves as marriage counselors, will work with couples, married or unmarried, heterosexual or homosexual.

The well-trained marriage counselor has a great deal of information to share about marital behavior, sexual practices, family planning, and the dynamics of interaction in couples. Marriage or couples counseling may be practiced by one person or by counselors working in pairs. The same is true of family counseling.

PASTORAL COUNSELOR. A pastoral counselor may be a nun, minister, priest or rabbi who has some training in social work or psychology. S/he may have a degree in one of the psychotherapy professions but is more likely to have received training at the convent or seminary, along with religious studies. Sometimes this training is extensive and helpful in preparing the counselor to handle emotional problems; sometimes the overlap with religious training may be so great that therapy is not viewed as a distinct discipline. Increasingly, though, pastoral counseling is becoming professionalized, with special training courses, journals, books and organizations.

Pastoral counselors are more likely than are many therapists to be outspoken on the issue of their own system of values. This can be positive if the counselor is also objective and democratic, but it can be very limiting when the counselor has narrow interests and an autocratic attitude. Many pastors are accustomed to being in a position of considerable power and authority when discussing values and personal problems. They may or may not be open-minded on such issues as sex, homosexuality, abortion, or out-of-wedlock children, according to the teachings of their religion.

STUDENT PSYCHOTHERAPIST

Most schools of clinical psychology, counseling, social work, or human services require that students have a placement, internship, or practicum in which they can work with clients and receive supervision from teachers or other therapists. Students are likely to work in community agencies or clinics where there are many clients and supervision available. Students usually work for little or no pay, but the agency may still charge the client a fee for their services.

If you interview a therapist who is a student, do not make the immediate assumption that s/he is unqualified. Psychotherapy students often have extensive background in related fields, or they may have been engaged in various kinds of counseling before they decided to go to school to get official credentials. Students are apt to be eager to help and to put in more hours with a client than graduate therapists; they may be more up-to-date in their therapy methods and information because they are currently taking courses; and they are not apt to be so set in their ways as a seasoned veteran. If you have an unusual problem or need special help, a student may be more willing to take a flexible approach.

The drawbacks of students are: they will be with an agency only for a limited time, perhaps leaving before you are ready to terminate; they may have limited hours free during the week because they are at the agency only during specific times; and they may be hesitant or awkward at times when you most need decisiveness. A student psychotherapist should be evaluated by the same standards you would apply to any other therapist: can you trust her/him, and are your goals in therapy being addressed.

Non-Medical Titles: Non-Specific

PSYCHOTHERAPIST

This is another general term like counselor, one that has no agreed-upon meaning and is not controlled by law. Practitioners from many backgrounds use it to indicate that they are specifically interested in working with clients on emotional and interpersonal issues. This is especially true when a person's professional title suggests something else, e.g., a person with a degree in sociology who has decided to specialize in psychotherapy may not want to use the misleading title sociologist. Psychotherapist is one of those titles that can be assumed by anyone, from the person with no credentials whatsoever to someone with many years of experience or training on a graduate level. Some alternative psychotherapy programs have been developed by institutes with no official standing. These institutes have sprung up in opposition to traditional schools and agencies which they see as having admission policies and requirements discriminatory toward women, Third World students, and poor people. People calling themselves psychotherapists may have graduated from one of these training programs, and you should feel free to investigate them.

MENTAL HEALTH WORKER, PARAPROFESSIONAL, COMMUNITY WORKER, STREET WORKER, HUMAN SERVICES WORKER, PSYCHIATRIC TECHNICIAN, VOLUNTEER

People with these titles have often received their training on the job or in short training programs. They work in clinics, half-way houses, alternative counseling agencies —anywhere where the pay is low and the hours undesirable. Their credentials may consist of an undergraduate degree in psychology, a two-year associate's degree from a community college, in-service training from the agency where they work, or extensive first-hand experience helping people with emotional problems. Some are students, while in other programs, paraprofessionals may perform administrative functions. Some of the titles are more descriptive of the type of work that people do: street workers often work out on the street with hard-to-reach kids. Often they do work that so-called professionals don't want to do or don't have to do anymore. Usually, none is licensed.

Just as you would with any therapist, be sure to consider what skills and capabilities a person using one of these titles has that can be useful to you. Many people feel that paraprofessionals may bring extra warmth and empathy to the therapy setting because they may have faced similar problems and may be willing to share their experiences. They may be more flexible at times and willing to work with clients in non-traditional ways.

FEMINIST THERAPIST

Like the terms psychotherapist or counselor, the term feminist therapist may refer to a woman* within any of the various psychotherapy fields. She specializes in the sociology and psychology of women and identifies herself as a feminist. She may have been trained in any of the various schools of therapy, but has probably examined the different theories with an eye for the sexism which often underlies them, attempting to feminize the techniques by keeping what is positive and useful for women.

Some feminist therapists restrict their practice to women, while others treat both men and women. Many run special interest groups for women, such as assertiveness training or mother-and-daughter groups. Some feminist therapists will indicate that they are particularly interested in, or skilled in, working with lesbians. Since

---

*A man is not a feminist therapist. He may be non-sexist or have worked on his own sexism, but we would regard as opportunism the motives of any man who wanted to call himself a feminist.

feminist therapist is a title that can be assumed by anyone, you need to do a further check on the particular background and interests of anyone using it.

SEX THERAPIST

Again, this title is not controlled by law and has no generally agreed-upon meaning. Sex therapy, perhaps more than any other field of therapy, is open to abuse by unqualified or unethical practitioners. If you consult someone about sexual problems, they should not offer to demonstrate sexual technique to you. Although legitimate sex therapists may use surrogate sexual partners in some cases, this is never undertaken lightly or without exhaustive consultation. Discussing sexuality in an open and frank way is often difficult, and you should expect that it may be hard for you, but a sex therapist should not press you for unnecessary detail.

The Masters and Johnson clinic in St. Louis has trained a number of therapists in different cities. These therapists may have received their earlier training in any of the disciplines we have already mentioned, such as social work, psychology, or medicine. Also, some hospitals or universities in large cities have special sex clinics attached to them. You might want to read a book like *Understanding Human Sexual Inadequacy* by Fred Belliveau and Lin Richter.[2] This is a paperback with an easily understandable explanation of the Masters and Johnson techniques, which can help you to evaluate a potential therapist.

NOTES

1. Fritz Redlich, M.D., and Stephen R. Kellert, M.D., "Trends in American Mental Health," *The American Journal of Psychiatry* 135:1, January 1978.

2. Fred Belliveau and Lin Richter, *Understanding Human Sexual Inadequacy.*

Chapter
10

Interviewing
a Therapist

Your personal interaction with your therapist is crucial to a successful experience in therapy. No matter how qualified or knowledgeable your therapist is, your therapy will not be as effective as it should be if you don't interact well with each other, and if you don't feel a sense of trust. It isn't the same as going to your gynecologist, for example, in which case personality is important only insofar as it helps the doctor convey and interpret necessary technical information to you. Clients in therapy are in a vulnerable position emotionally because they are confiding problems and feelings to someone whom they need to trust and depend on. This requires confidence that the therapist won't abuse that trust. A woman who had recently terminated therapy reports, "Therapy worked for me because of the interaction and trust between myself and my therapist. I felt like she really cared about my welfare."

How can you choose a therapist who will be helpful to you? You need to know more about a therapist than whether or not s/he has the proper credentials. There are at least three important considerations in choosing a therapist: (1) *credentials* (training and experience, see Chapter 9), (2) *orientation* (type of therapy practiced, see Chapters 4–7), and (3) *personality*. You can obtain information on credentials and orientation from the therapist right away, even over the phone (see Appendix A on how to locate a therapist). A therapist should be willing to spend a few minutes on the phone to tell you something about her/his availability, fees, and perhaps training or areas of special interest. Information on personality, however, requires that you *interview* the therapist, meaning that you arrange a meeting to ask questions and evaluate for yourself the answers and your own reactions. We cannot emphasize enough that information about credentials and training is not sufficient to enable you to choose a therapist.

Interviewing your therapist helps to establish that you are a person who is deciding whether or not to purchase a service, not a patient who has to accept just any treatment offered. A woman entering therapy has definite rights, and it is legitimate to ask your therapist questions and expect honest, personal answers. Being in therapy does not mean you are sick or crazy. You are the consumer paying for a service, just as you are when you hire a lawyer or consult a doctor.

Interviewing the Therapist

We recommend that you interview your therapist during the first session. You may find it helpful to see two or three therapists for one session each so that you can compare styles. If you do this, be sure to ask if you will have to pay for this hour (usually called an *intake* or *consultation*). In the first session the therapist will usually ask you questions about your immediate situation, history, and feelings. During this session you can also ask her/him questions. In this way you can make sure you are both starting therapy with similar expectations.

Sometimes just the manner in which your questions are answered and discussed will be more important than the content of the answers. For example, a therapist may respond to a question with "Why do you want to know?" Sometimes this is legitimate and as such deserves an answer; but it can also be used to avoid answering your questions. If the therapist seems to be doing this, try to point it out. If you are uncomfortable with this style, you can find a therapist who is more direct.

If you are in crisis when you enter therapy and unable to assert your rights or conduct an interview, you may decide later that this therapist is not the person you would want to do long-term work with. Try to arrange to bring a friend to the first session if you are, indeed, in crisis. This is a legitimate option and one you should feel free to discuss with your therapist.

If you have been assigned a therapist in a clinic, you may run into difficulty if you want to consult someone else; you may be told that any client can work with any therapist so you must be resisting therapy. Chances are, it is the clinic staff that is resistant to the inconvenience of finding you a new therapist. It is important to remember that you are the consumer. You have the right to shop around for your therapist and to interview several people if you wish. Going into therapy may entail making a large personal and financial investment; if your reaction to a particular therapist is basically negative, look for someone else before you make these investments.

Questions You Can Use in an Interview

Where do the therapist's ideas come from? What is her/his training?

What style of therapy does s/he use? Will your therapy be conducted in the same style as the initial interview?

What type of therapy does s/he think you need? Does s/he feel s/he will be able to work with you in this way? How long will therapy take?

What are the therapist's ideas about a mentally healthy woman?

What are the therapist's views on homosexuality or bisexuality?

Will the therapist prescribe medication? What are her/his attitudes about this and about hospitalization?

What will the fee be? How will this be determined?

Will the therapist be available weekends, or evenings, or for extra sessions?

Are there other times when you can call her/him at the office or at home?

The Purpose of the Interview

The interview can give you an impression of the sensitivity of the therapist. When a therapist is authoritarian and insensitive to the anxieties and nervousness often experienced by women in initial interviews, ineffective therapy will probably be the result. Impressive credentials might make you feel in awe of the therapist, leading to feelings of helplessness or inadequacy. A good therapist will help you to overcome these feelings by not placing undue emphasis on her/his credentials and by trying to make you feel more comfortable.

The interview will help you evaluate the therapist's techniques. Ask the therapist how s/he would treat a certain problem. Then decide whether you would feel comfortable with that approach and if it would be effective for you.

A psychoanalyst, for example, might expect the patient to "resolve her transference neurosis," meaning that she no longer assign to her therapist feelings and attitudes that were originally associated with important childhood figures (such as parents or siblings). The Rogerian therapist seeks to promote the client's spontaneity and creativity by helping her tap into her inner resources. A behaviorist might look no further than to eliminating an annoying "symptom." If your goal is to overcome your shyness and be able to meet more people, and your therapist's goal is to delve into your unconscious for childhood traumas, the chances are you will not be happy with that therapist unless you can come to some agreement about the focus of therapy.

Another reason for the interview is to get a sense of the therapist's values. You want to be sure your therapist's goals for you coincide with your own expectations of therapy. Try to get a sense of how the therapist feels about women. Many therapists have destructive ideas about normal female behavior. You can ask a therapist directly to tell you her/his notions of a mentally healthy woman, and hope that this will elicit an honest statement of the therapist's politics and therapeutic ideas. Set ideas on whether or not women should be married, should be involved with a man, should have children, or should have a career are all often indicators of stereotypical thinking; and you don't want to be stereotyped. You also want to avoid the therapist who doesn't take your problems seriously, or who doesn't take women's problems seriously.

Evaluating the Interview—Issues to Consider

After the interview, evaluate how the therapist answered your questions. If you know someone who has been in therapy, you could discuss your reactions with her. The following ideas may be helpful to you in thinking about these issues.

PERSONALITY

Studies indicate that some people are better therapists than others simply because of their personalities. This kind of a therapeutic personality seems to be a key to client improvement or deterioration. Regardless of whether someone is a social worker, psychologist, nurse, minister, psychiatrist, or teacher, if that person possesses certain personality traits, s/he will be more effective in interpersonal relationships. Furthermore, whether the therapist's orientation is feminist, Rogerian, or Freudian, s/he will be helpful in her/his efforts if s/he has these characteristics of the effective therapist. If s/he lacks them, s/he will probably be ineffective at best or even harmful, no matter what your problem is.

Your own intuitive feeling as to whether or not you are comfortable with a therapist is your best guide. There are several personality characteristics of the effective therapist that you can also keep in mind. One quality is *empathy,* which is the ability to accurately perceive what another person is experiencing and to communicate that perception. An empathic person facilitates communication, while the non-empathic person interferes with, or detracts from, communication.

Genuineness is also important. It is the ability of a person to be free from pretense, affectation, or hypocrisy. A genuine person is sincerely her/himself, not phony or overly defensive; there is no discrepancy between what s/he says and what s/he is experiencing. A person who is not genuine may say one thing and communicate another non-verbally. S/he may be stiffly professional or be playing a role, hiding behind a facade.

An effective therapist has the knack of keeping communication *relevant* and *concrete.* S/he deals with your specific feelings and experiences, exploring them in depth. S/he does not allow you to avoid or escape the issues at hand. A less effective therapist is more abstract or general and allows you to go off on tangents. At the same time, a good therapist accepts that you have the right to make your own decisions and live your own life. S/he *respects* your dignity as a human being and is not overly protective, condescending, or a bully.

A good therapist is not afraid to *confront* you when s/he sees a discrepancy between what you are saying and what you seem to be experiencing, or what you are saying at one point and what you have said before. Initiating a confrontation is risky, since it sometimes precipitates a crisis, but this is often what it takes to promote growth both in and out of therapy. Another characteristic of a good therapist, which is also risky, is *personal disclosure,* or the sharing of information from her/his personal life. This communicates to you that your therapist is not perfect and also helps to equalize the power inequality that tends to exist in therapy. An ineffective therapist is either cold and aloof, or uses the therapy situation to meet her/his own needs rather than yours by confiding information inappropriately.

The relationship between you and your therapist should be *warm* and *alive.* Your therapist should be able to communicate verbally and non-verbally (but *not* sexually) that s/he appreciates you. This needs to be done in an appropriate way, which will depend on what you are comfortable with. One of the most important aspects of therapy is being able to work out problems in an ongoing, interpersonal relationship. You should feel comfortable in learning to confront, to reveal yourself, and to safely express negative or positive emotions to another person. This is possible when you know that your therapist is concerned and appreciates you as a person, and when the therapist feels comfortable in exploring and discussing the relationship that exists between the two of you.

Finally, an effective therapist is *dynamic* and *self-confident,* able to communicate a sense of competence and *security* to her/his clients. S/he can serve as a model of someone who is not incapacitated by stress and tension, and who can be flexible and open rather than judgmental or rigid. The therapeutic relationship can be seen as a model of communication and expression of feelings between two people. This relationship evolves toward greater equality as the therapy grows and eventually terminates.

TRAINING AND CREDENTIALS

Considering all the various credentials and backgrounds a therapist might have (see Chapter 9), how can you best judge which is most appropriate to your needs? This is a difficult question to answer, and we can only give some very general guidelines for you to go by.

SEVERITY OF YOUR PROBLEM. When a woman comes to therapy wanting to gain a deeper understanding of herself and insight into her experience as a woman, to learn helpful skills, such as assertiveness, or to feel more alive and competent in the world, this is generally called *personal growth work*. The type of therapist qualified to do this kind of work is someone who has extensive practical experience working with various groups of people, but who may or may not have extensive formal education. S/he may have attended therapy workshops or a certificate program at a therapy training institute. Her/his personality and flexibility will be very important.

If a woman feels depressed or unable to cope with the stress in her life, she should seek a therapist with some formal training in psychotherapy, at least at a Master's degree level, because the nature of her problem is more pressing and requires more than personal growth work, as well as a more technical understanding of certain clinical skills.

If a woman is in severe distress, she may feel that she needs to consult someone with access to medication or hospitalization. This must be a psychiatrist, although some non-physician psychotherapists do work in conjunction with psychiatrists.

The need does exist in certain emergency situations for a therapist with medical training. There is some question, however, of whether psychiatrists are effective with long-term psychotherapy. Medical school training has generally encouraged an attitude of aloofness, superiority, and authoritarianism which is useful to a doctor who needs to have a tremendous amount of self-confidence and needs to remain objective about the physical suffering s/he must deal with. But therapy isn't medicine and in fact requires the opposite sort of attitude—warmth, empathy, and genuineness.

YOUR DEGREE OF COMFORT. You should try to interview at least two therapists so you can evaluate their credentials in relation to your needs. You can also consider the degree of formality with which you are comfortable. Remember to be aware of whether the therapist's office is fully equipped with desk, leather couch, and a secretary or simply with plants and pillows on the floor. This may give you some indication of the therapist's style and of how comfortable you will feel in therapy.

HAS THE THERAPIST EVER BEEN A CLIENT? Ask the therapist if s/he has personally been in therapy as part of her/his training. The reasons that s/he should have been are important. First, being a client her/himself at some point increases your therapist's ability to empathize with you. Knowing how it feels to be afraid to look at something or admit to certain feelings gives a therapist greater sensitivity in her/his work.

Personal therapy also helps therapists deal with the emotional strains of their work. Therapy involves intense emotional encounters wherein your therapist is not only absorbed with your problems but often takes the brunt of your feelings, such as anger and frustration. Rather than becoming defensive or blaming her/himself, your therapist must make the interaction a productive one. This requires inner strength, a sense of self-worth, and an ability to deal with stress. Therapists who are aware of other people's struggles need to be aware of their own and work on them. A therapist who has been in therapy knows that clients are not sick and that therapists are not superior beings.

ORIENTATION

There are several different styles of therapy, the basic categories being verbal, experiential, directive, and behavioral. Some women are not concerned about working with a particular technique. Others prefer therapists with skills in specific areas, such as psychodrama or bioenergetics. If you feel that a particular approach will be most effective for you, by all means ask for it. However, be skeptical of therapists who are only into one so-called style. Therapists who are stuck on one way of working (like therapists who routinely prescribe drugs) are less likely to be skilled in dealing with a variety of problems. A good therapist will be familiar with several ways of working, so that s/he can suggest which would be most appropriate for you.

You need to know whether this first interview is indicative of the way the therapist usually works. If you are looking for a particular technique which the therapist says s/he uses, you may have to invest in several sessions, since the first interview tends to focus mainly on information you must tell your therapist about yourself.

SEXUAL PREFERENCE

Whether or not the therapist's sexual preference is a consideration in making your choice should depend on what

areas you will be working on in therapy. It is a consideration however, which can especially affect a lesbian client
who may prefer to work with a lesbian therapist, since you
should not have to spend time in your therapy educating
a therapist about your lifestyle. Even when the subject of
sexuality is not uppermost in the therapy, you may want
to work with a therapist who has more than an intellectual
understanding of your lifestyle and the issues surrounding
it.

Heterosexual therapists who received their training
from people hostile to lesbians may be prejudiced against
lesbians. Many therapists (both gay and straight) who are
feminists, however, have made a point of examining their
prejudices and have tried to resolve them for themselves.
You have the right to make this issue a priority.

The sexual preference of my therapist is important to me. My
relationship with the man I live with is important to me, and I
like knowing that my therapist has a good marriage—she's a
good role model. I might feel tense dealing with my relationships
with men with a lesbian therapist—maybe not.

I think the sexual preference of the therapist affects the relationship. I trust lesbians more to understand and not change me to
conform to the (hetero) system.

RACE AND CLASS

It is an unfortunate fact that, at this time, most non-white
or foreign-born women in this country will have trouble
locating a therapist with a racial and/or ethnic background similar to their own. This is also true for working-
class women, although probably not to the same extent.
Therapists tend to be white and middle-class, and their
first-hand knowledge of, or experience with, other groups
may be limited to what they have read (and not much is
available, for example, on Black women in therapy). Just
as a great many women feel that they are raised in a differ-

ent culture from men because of their separate roles, women of different races also have vastly different experiences in this culture.

Class prejudice can be the most subtle of all. Differences of economic status may skew the assumptions your therapist makes about what kind of life you live. For example, a middle- or upper-class therapist who can afford full-time household help may have trouble relating to the fact that a single parent supporting herself on a secretary's wage cannot manage to attend night school.

You will have to use your interview to evaluate whether or not a particular therapist is understanding enough to accept your own evaluation of your experience. Be sure to ask what experience the therapist has had of working with various different groups of people. Finally, try to evaluate whether the therapist holds values contradictory to your own by comparing, for example, lifestyles or education.

Male Therapists

We feel that the most effective therapists for women are women who can serve as models of competence and self-respect, autonomy, and a sense of responsibility to other women. Even the best male therapist can never be a role model for women clients. In the words of one woman who had been in therapy with a man: "I might have moved faster in therapy with a woman. I felt very inhibited with a man. Also I was looking for someone to identify with, and this was more complicated with a man."

However, there is no question that a good male therapist is a better choice than a sexist female therapist or a female therapist who has anti-male feelings which may potentially distort her client's views. To quote another woman who had been in therapy with a woman: "Possibly a *very* clear man could be a good therapist for women, able to help women deal with our conditioned responses to men.

I know male therapists who are good in some ways but limited in others—they have a certain rigidity although they are loving people."

Many women who answered our questionnaire reported problems with male therapists. One felt that "my therapist couldn't understand my fear of/anger toward men as much as I needed him to. I feel like I haven't been helped with this as much as I need to be, particularly after paying all that money." Along a similar vein, another said, "My therapist was the 'guru,' I was the 'learner,' and he never helped me see that a lot of what I was feeling is shared by lots of women. I felt isolated, alone, and alienated a lot!"

If you do interview a man, try to determine if he is sexist by asking him. If he doesn't know what you're talking about, the chances are he is! The following is a brief description of traits we feel that a male therapist should possess to work effectively with women clients.

A good male therapist must be knowledgeable about women's problems. This knowledge can be acquired through reading, discussion with female colleagues and clients, special courses on women's issues, or supervision from a woman therapist. He will be aware of his own values regarding male and female roles and believe that there should be no prescribed sex-role behaviors. He will not try to pressure a woman into valuing marriage and family over those lifestyle choices usually reserved for men. He rejects theories of behavior based on anatomical differences, such as those propounded by Freud or Erik Erikson, and he rejects the idea that lesbians are emotionally or sexually maladjusted. He would encourage his women clients to be assertive and autonomous, just as he would encourage his male clients to be sensitive and nurturing.

There are a few situations[1] involving male therapists that you should try to avoid if possible. Avoid any women's group led by a man, since this only reinforces the role model of a powerful male to whom the women are subservient. It would also potentially set up a situation of competition for male attention, which would alienate the women from each other as sources of support. Avoid working with a man if your primary problem is marital difficulties, separation, or divorce. It is very easy to become dependent on a supportive male therapist as a way of separating from a lover, and then be unable to terminate therapy unless another relationship of dependence comes along.

If you are hostile to men, don't feel that you have to work with one in order to resolve the issue—that's the long way around. An easier solution would be to work first with a woman, and then at some point join a mixed-sex group. If you have trouble relating to men in anything but a seductive manner, you would be well-advised to work with a woman or join a women's group. When women develop close relationships with each other and increase their self-esteem, they no longer have to feel dependent on the approval of men and can learn to relate to them in healthier ways.

Practical Considerations

When you interview a therapist, there are a few technical details to be sure to ask about. These include fees, the availability of your therapist, and how long you can expect to be in therapy.

FEES

The fee is the amount of money you pay for a therapist's time, attention, and responsibility to you. Before or during the initial interview with the therapist, it is important to settle on a fee which is acceptable to both of you.

Therapists either charge a flat rate or negotiate the fee. Some negotiate within a specific price range, called a sliding scale, in which you are not asked to pay more than you can realistically afford. Some agencies also adjust their fees according to what you can afford, so be sure to explain your financial situation fully. If you happen to go to a community mental health center or multiservice agency where you do not have to pay, remember that this does not mean that you or your therapist won't take therapy seriously. We believe that negotiating the fee to the satisfaction of both you and your therapist is the fairest way to handle the matter. You should not be forced to pay a flat rate, particularly over $35, if you simply cannot afford it. Therapy does not have to cost a lot to be effective. *Don't be fooled by high prices;* they are not necessarily an indication of quality.

THERAPIST AVAILABILITY

Another detail you may want to cover in the interview is how available the therapist is in emergencies. You can ask if s/he is willing to schedule extra sessions or see you in the evening or on weekends. You can also ask if s/he takes phone calls at home. You will want to be clear about what can be expected of your relationship, especially when you are in crisis.

LENGTH OF TREATMENT

The length of time you spend in therapy will depend on the severity of your problem. If you are working on personal growth, steer clear of the therapist who tries to sell long-term therapy (over one year). If you feel you have serious or incapacitating problems, be wary of the therapist with quick solutions or easy answers. Finally, you have the right to decide how much time you want to spend in therapy. It is perfectly legitimate to focus on an immediate problem or decision and choose not to spend time on more complex, deep-rooted issues.

Evaluating the Interview—Questions to Ask Yourself

Did you feel comfortable?

Did the therapist make it easy for you to talk about your reasons for coming to therapy?

Did s/he seem to understand what you were talking about?

How were your questions answered? Openly and honestly? Defensively?

What was asked of you?

Did you and the therapist agree on goals and expectations of therapy? Did s/he see your problems the way you do?

Did you trust the therapist or feel that trust would grow in time?

Were you taken seriously?

Was the therapist sincere, responsive and genuinely concerned?

Do you feel you share basic values, such as what constitutes a healthy woman?

If you want to make, or have already made, unconventional lifestyle choices, how did the therapist react to these?

Are you satisfied with the way the fee was negotiated?

Options After the Interview

You have several options after interviewing a therapist. You might feel so positive that you decide on the spot to continue. Similarly, you may feel so negative that you know you don't want to come back. Often, however, women have mixed feelings and need time to evaluate their impressions before making a decision. Some want to interview one or two other therapists before deciding. Even if you do continue, you have the option to leave at any time. Therapy is a continuous interviewing process as you learn whether or not you can trust the therapist.

You don't have to decide anything on the spot. Tell the therapist you will call her/him if you decide to continue. Even if you feel uncomfortable giving a therapist negative feedback about an interview, try to do so. Most therapists will appreciate learning that they don't need to hold an opening in their schedules or wait for your call.

As you consider your interview, rememeber that therapy is something you do for *yourself.* A woman who has been in therapy on two different occasions suggests: "Be committed to it. Don't spend your time in idle philosophizing and *don't* ask your therapist for the answers. She doesn't know, and if she claims to, she's not doing her job properly. Don't let other people's experiences in therapy determine what you think you should be doing or how fast it should be going. Everyone is different. Don't feel discouraged if things start slowly or you seem to be in a slump. Eventually it'll pick up again. And have certain goals in mind when you start. It's impossible to get anywhere when you don't know where you're going. Most importantly, you must really want to do it."

NOTES

1. Edna Rawlings and Diane Carter, "Feminist and Nonsexist Psychotherapy," *Psychotherapy for Women,* Rawlings and Carter, eds., pp. 71–2.

Chapter 11

Your Relationship with Your Therapist

Psychotherapy is above all the relationship between you and your therapist. The nature of this relationship varies widely, depending on the style of therapy that is employed and the personality and values of both you and your therapist. There is a certain type of relationship, particularly effective for women. This is similar to what has been described as effective therapy for women (Chapter 2), Feminist Therapy (Chapter 5), and the therapeutic personality (Chapter 10).

Because the therapy relationship is structured (unlike friendship), each person has certain legitimate expectations of, and obligations to, the other. Your therapist will expect you to come for your sessions, present material for therapy, and pay a mutually agreed-upon fee. What you can expect of your therapist, however, is not always so clear.

Therapy is a service that one person performs for another, like medicine or law. When you hire a therapist to provide this personal service for you, a contract is implied, although not often acknowledged. The gist of this implied contract is that the therapist is working in good faith for your best interests and would do nothing to deliberately hurt you, e.g., force treatment on you against your will or behave unethically in any way.

Viewing therapy in this light, you can expect your therapist to have certain skills which you do not have and which you are willing to purchase. Your therapist should show professional discretion and a disciplined unconcern with matters not vital to the therapy. S/he should be civil and respectful. You have a right to expect your therapist to take an intense, albeit temporary, interest in you, in terms of your own best interests.

Some therapists have an inflated idea of the dignity of their role. These therapists may remain aloof and have a preconceived idea of what their clients' best interests are rather than listening to what the client is asking for. In this way some therapists perpetuate the current values and norms of society by imposing them on their clients. Other schools of therapy break down the traditional inequality of the therapist/client hierarchy. Feminist therapy, for example, encourages the therapist to share information about her life and her values, when appropriate. The client is encouraged to give negative as well as positive feedback to the therapist concerning the therapy process, goals, and values, and is helped to realize that she, the client, is the consumer who can shop, question, and evaluate, as she does in any other service relationship.

Ideally, your therapist should not abuse the power of her/his position. S/he has the responsibility to not take advantage of your inherent vulnerability as the person seeking help. Even though your therapist may be the expert in a special field, you as the client have the power either to stay with this particular therapist or to seek help elsewhere.

Women have particular difficulty taking power or using the power they have for several reasons. Most women are not accustomed to having power in their own lives, and their tendency, especially when in distress, is to not challenge anyone who seems to be an expert. Women have also been conditioned to not take full responsibility for themselves but instead to rely on a relationship to support them. Finally, since most therapists are men, there is an inclination in both client and male therapist to duplicate the one up/one down relationship (where one person, usually the man, is clearly dominant and one, usually the woman, is subordinate) that commonly exists between men and women in this society.

We feel that possibly *the* most important aspect of therapy for a woman is experiencing herself as an equal to someone she respects. This does not mean that there is no difference between the roles you and your therapist take, and there will be times when you feel weak and needful of a stronger person. What equality in therapy does mean is that you and your therapist respect each other as worthwhile people. There are many different ways in which an effective therapist for women can promote this equality in the therapy relationship.

I see the therapist/client relationship as hopefully equals with *different* roles. Sharing is extremely important both as how we respond to each other and in the way of sharing histories.

I have received much support and constructive criticism and have been helped to see some behavior patterns. I have been treated as a responsible person able to make decisions.

What Makes a Good Therapy Relationship?

If, in your relationship with your therapist, you are given responsibility for yourself and are encouraged to respect your feelings, take charge of your life, and be aware of the process by which you give up your power and allow others to have power over you, you can begin to experience your own strength. When this happens, your therapist becomes

less a leader or director and more a vehicle or catalyst for
change.

Therapists who work effectively with women are sensitive to the ways in which they can abuse their power, and
they will use any of several therapeutic strategies to bal-
ance the client/therapist relationship[1]:

• The therapist is open about what her/his values are,
particularly those relating to women's role in society. If
the therapist is a woman, she relates these values to her
own personal experience. Because she can share, when-
ever appropriate, her feelings, frustrations, failures, and
triumphs, the therapist can be a realistic role model for
her clients.

• The therapist takes what you say at face value. Not only
does s/he *believe* you, but s/he does not belittle you with
obscure or complicated interpretations. S/he shares her
impressions in a non-judgmental way. If you contradict
yourself in some way, the therapist simply points it out or
asks you for your own interpretation.

• The therapist doesn't make decisions for you or tell you
what to do. Most women are struggling to learn how to take
responsibility for themselves and need to learn how to
respect their own decisions. Being told what to do puts you
in a childlike position and is not psychotherapy (the exception being a situation in which you are emotionally
incapable of making any decision at all and need some
guidance until you are no longer in crisis).

• The therapist assumes that you are the expert on yourself. S/he respects your decisions, and therapy proceeds at
your own pace. A therapist should not promote the illusion
that s/he is omniscient or knows more about you than you
know about yourself. This is often done in the guise of
encouraging the transference, in fact encouraging you to
experience yourself as a child.

- Therapy is demystified by sharing skills. The therapist can teach you how to be your own therapist in this way. S/he tells you what s/he is doing and why, and respects your decision to refuse a new technique. Some of the techniques women have learned from therapy include assertiveness skills, dream analysis, decision-making skills, and the art of constructive criticism.

- The therapist encourages feedback and criticism. If you are dissatisfied with some aspect of therapy, it's important that you feel comfortable to say so. If you are angry with your therapist or feel s/he has made a mistake, you need not fear that you will be punished and called resistant. If the therapist feels that s/he has made a mistake, s/he admits it.

- The therapist encourages you to become less dependent on therapy by getting involved in your community. Therapy has to extend beyond the four walls of the therapist's office. Women can eliminate their sense of isolation by participating in women's groups, taking classes, or becoming active politically. If a woman feels she can work with others to change the social system, she will have the experience of being a powerful, effective person.

- Diagnoses or diagnostic testing are not relied upon. They put the therapist in the expert position because the tests are usually hard to understand or interpret. It is a point of controversy among therapists whether diagnoses of so-called mental illness are in any way accurate. Diagnostic labels are particularly oppressive because they are so derogatory. Lesbians, for example, have suffered from being labeled as sexual deviants.

Therapists who use diagnoses tend to see clients as fitting certain categories rather than as individuals. Studies indicate that therapists who rely on diagnoses tend to label whatever their clients do as a symptom of their "illness" and distort their life histories to support the diagnosis. Medical training in particular predisposes a therapist toward an interpretation of "illness" and a tendency toward diagnostic conformity with other "experts," rather than an impression specific to the client herself.

• You should have access to your records, if any are kept. Being told that you would be disturbed by seeing your records makes therapy unnecessarily mysterious and reinforces the power of the therapist.

• The focus of therapy is on action and problem-solving, rather than introspection. You are urged to recognize the power you have to make changes in your own life, and consequently the power you have within the therapy relationship itself. If, for example, a woman is angry about being exploited at work, one approach open to her might be to explore her failure to assert herself effectively on the job, her unrealistic expectations of employment, or her masochism in staying in the job. The implication of this approach is that the individual is responsible as the sole source of her problem. A different focus would be to encourage the woman to feel her anger, recognize its validity, and give it verbal expression. Anger is a source of energy that can be used constructively to change a situation and doesn't necessarily need to be worked through or dissipated. The woman might do such things as file a complaint, circulate a petition, confront her boss, organize a strike, or leave the job if all else fails. Nothing she does should leave her feeling defeated or humiliated. If she does have masochistic feelings that inhibit her from fighting for her rights, then the therapist can explore her history to discover the roots of the problem. This history is social as well as personal and familial, and includes things like what kinds of submissive behavior were taught to the woman in school. We believe this approach to be the most effective for women.

The Therapy Contract

As a client, you are in a vulnerable position in the therapy relationship because of the distress you are experiencing and because of your inexperience of therapy. One way by which you can initiate a more equal participation is to work out a contract with your therapist. Since not all therapists are familiar with the concept of a contract, however, you will probably have to be the one to suggest it.

A contract is a verbal or written agreement regarding the goals and operating procedures of therapy. This agreement is arrived at by both you and your therapist; it is not dictated by one to the other. There is never any guarantee or promise that therapy will be successful, but a contract will clarify and define what you intend to work on and what your therapist takes responsibility for. Another asset of a contract is its demystification of both of your roles. A contract makes your relationship more equal because it is based on mutual consent.

The contract should be reviewed periodically (probably every month or two), since your problems and goals may change. Therapy is a process, as much as it is a means to an end; both you and your therapist have an obligation to be aware of the process and not let it get bogged down or off on the wrong track. The contract also gives you a tool for evaluating your therapist and deciding whether or not s/he is doing her/his job.

A contract should cover the following points:

THERAPY GOALS Many women come to therapy without any specific goals in mind. They may be depressed and unhappy, having problems with relationships, or feeling that their lives are unfulfilled. Therapists, on the other hand, almost always have goals in mind for their clients. These goals could be anything from adjusting the client to her feminine role to resolving a transference neurosis to helping her become a feminist.

You can ask your therapist for help in clarifying your goals if you are unable to be specific about them yourself. You should expect your therapist to be open about her/his goals and to be as specific as possible about them. If your goals and those of the therapist are not compatible, you should end the relationship.

Agreeing on goals helps ensure that therapy will proceed in a certain direction without any hidden agendas. One woman, who felt that the goal-setting process was important, expressed it this way:

What was positive about my therapy relationship was setting up goals and an approximate time period to achieve these goals at the start of therapy. Realizing from the beginning that the therapist was there to guide or assist me but that I would be dealing with and working out my own problems was important to me. There was never a feeling of dependency on the therapist.

The contract is flexible and can be re-evaluated at any time and changed if you want to focus on new issues. This review is usually informal and can consist of no more than looking at what has been accomplished and what still needs to be worked on. For example, a woman's initial goal might be to understand why she is depressed. As the sources of her depression become clear, she might decide to focus on learning to be assertive in her job or perhaps deciding whether or not to leave her marriage.

THERAPY METHODS It would be helpful for you to decide in advance whether verbal, experiential, or directive therapy is best suited to your needs. You have the right to refuse any method that you have not agreed on. You should also agree on whether you want individual, couple, or group therapy. Are these options available to you if you decide you need them? Discuss with your therapist whether or not s/he prescribes medication. This is particularly important if the therapist is a psychiatrist. Like goals, therapy methods can change as therapy progresses.

THERAPY ARRANGEMENTS It is important to establish in the initial interviews exactly when you will be coming to therapy—could the hour be changed if your schedule does, how many times a week will you meet and for how long (fifty minutes; one hour)? Would your therapist be available to meet you for an emergency session if that were necessary? Is s/he available for phone calls?

FEES One of the most important areas to agree on with your therapist is fees. Do not accept a therapist who delegates all responsibility for fees to a secretary or other person in the office; this therapist will probably not be open to talking about or negotiating fees, should it later become a problem.

Many therapists are eligible to accept insurance payments—not only psychiatrists, but also licensed psychologists, social workers, or therapists working with someone who is licensed. If you have any type of insurance, check your policy to see if it includes coverage for mental health care; and be sure to ask if you can use it.

Confidentiality

You should be aware that whether you go to a private therapist or to a social service agency, clinic, or hospital, information about you may be shared in several ways. Most commonly, in agencies or hospitals, records are kept of all pertinent facts about you and of all the meetings or phone calls with your therapist, including her/his opinion, or diagnosis, of you. Depending on the strictness of the agency and the industry of your therapist, the records might be very detailed or relatively vague.

In agencies or hospitals records are routinely seen by secretarial help, supervisors, consultants, and other therapists. These people may not be particularly interested in your records, but the records are there to be seen if they do decide to look. Your record will also be passed on if you change therapists or if you come back to the agency after even a long absence. If there is information in your record which you feel may be harmful to you, try to deal with it before it is passed on. In Massachusetts, for example, a recent law gives patients the right to see their psychiatric records, although a hospital or doctor may withhold them if a patient is currently in treatment or if seeing the records would be "detrimental" to the patient's mental health. In other states, where a client has no legal recourse, it may seem impossible for you to see your records. However, you can give permission for your records to be sent to a doctor of your choice who may allow you easier access to what has been written about you. Many patient groups are working to change the laws to allow easier access to records.

Private therapists have more leeway than agencies have in what information goes into the records they keep. Be sure to ask your therapist what kind of records s/he keeps, who sees them and for what reason, and who else might have access to them. Many private therapists have supervisors who may review their records or get a verbal accounting of them; or perhaps they use a group supervision method with partners or collective members. Find out if your therapist shares client information with other people and, if so, if pseudonyms are used for the client's protection. If the therapist uses a tape recorder, find out why, who will hear the tape, and whether or not the tape will eventually be destroyed.

There are good reasons for therapists to discuss their cases with each other. They may be looking for a new perspective on a client's situation, for information about a particular problem, or for resources for a client. However, you should be able to expect your therapist not to engage in casual gossip about you or reveal information about you without your signed consent. If you want your therapist to share information about you with another agency, a lawyer, or your spouse, give her/him written permission stating specifically to whom the information can be given. Do not sign a general consent form which would allow the information to be given to anyone.

There are also good reasons to want more privacy or confidentiality than is usual. You might have a friend or relative who works in the agency where you are being treated; you might have several friends also seeing your therapist; your therapist might be friendly with a number of people you know in the community. Any of these might be reasons for you to be extra sure to check with your therapist about confidentiality. Agencies will often make provisions for your records to be filed under a pseudonym to ensure your privacy.

Legally, a client/therapist privilege (protecting the therapist from having to testify in court or give access to records) has been held to exist only between M.D.'s and their patients. Every state varies in its laws, and you have to check your own state about this. Generally, this privilege means that if it is important to you that some information you share in therapy be kept out of the record, you should discuss this with your therapist beforehand and be sure you both agree that it not be written down. If you think your therapist might be subpoenaed to testify in any legal case involving you, the question of records and what information your therapist retains is very important.

Feelings

The feelings clients have about therapists, and vice versa, are as varied as the feelings between any two people and can range from friendship, anger, trust, frustration, respect, ad infinitum. Some therapists choose to focus more on these feelings than others do. Most forms of therapy acknowledge the significance of the feelings between client and therapist.

Freudian (or analytic) therapists, for example, call the feelings the client has toward the therapist transference, and the feelings the therapist has for the client counter-transference. Freud believed that these feelings were projections of feelings originally directed toward other significant people, usually parents. The purpose of analytic therapy is to come to understand these feelings and no longer be a victim of them. Interpersonal therapy views the relationship between client and therapist as a model of how the client relates to other people in her life. The therapist's job is to interpret unrealistic distortions the client may make. Existential therapists, without any interpretation, simply work with and guide the relationship as it develops. In group therapy, much time is spent focusing on the feelings group members have toward each other as a way for each member to understand how she relates to other people.

Your feelings about your therapist are an important clue to whether or not therapy is going to be a positive experience for you. Basically, you should expect to trust your therapist, to feel confident that s/he is working in your best interests, and to respect her/his technical skill. These feelings should be present most of the time; however, even in a positive relationship, it is not unusual to have some negative feelings. Sometimes you will disagree with your therapist's handling of a situation; sometimes you will be resistant, indicating that the therapy is forcing you to deal with something unpleasant or to face an aspect of yourself which you would rather avoid. Some symptoms of this resistance may include being late for your appointments or cancelling them altogether, refusing to discuss certain issues, or feeling dissatisfied with the therapist for the same reasons that you feel dissatisfied with other people in your life.

My therapy went *a lot* faster than I expected—that was nice. But I never realized that it was so much hard work and that progress on certain subjects would proceed so slowly—sometimes it seemed I was getting nowhere, when in fact things *were* moving.

I felt a serious commitment and was conscious of "being in therapy" twenty-four hours a day, not just one hour a week.

If you feel generally satisfied with your therapy, but find yourself experiencing any of the above symptoms, try to discuss your feelings with your therapist and work them through. There are some situations, however, that indicate that the relationship is a negative one. Pay attention to your feelings; discuss them with friends whose judgment you trust. If you run into one or more of the following problems, you should seriously consider changing therapists.

• You don't like your therapist as a person. S/he may strike you as cold and aloof, or too critical, or syrupy sweet. Whatever the cause, there is no reason for you to have to overcome an initial dislike—therapy is difficult enough as it is. Remember, though, that this situation is different from liking your therapist at first and later changing your mind; that usually indicates resistance.

• The therapist is rude and inconsiderate. This might be apparent in such behavior as her/his taking phone calls during the session, writing notes about something else, or even falling asleep! You may have the impression the therapist isn't listening to you. Tell the therapist how you are feeling, but don't waste a lot of time waiting for her/him to change. If you feel your therapist does not respect you, you should switch therapists.

• Your values conflict with those of the therapist. This will usually be obvious in the initial interview when you ask questions about the nature of mental health for women. Sexism is not the only possible conflict, though. Racism and classism might be problems, too. You may end up with a therapist of a different race or ethnic background from your own. If so, s/he should be able to acknowledge some lack of understanding of your experience. Classism means a lack of respect for or an inability to understand people of a different socio-economic background. It is important for therapists to have an open mind about different lifestyles as well and not be too rigidly conservative or radical. Be wary of someone who says her/his method works for everyone and transcends all differences.

• You feel your therapist is trying to force you into a mold. S/he might be telling you what to do or making decisions for you. S/he might only want to discuss certain topics and ignore others. S/he might openly or subtly approve of you for behaving in a certain way. Give the therapist feedback on this if you can, because s/he is likely to be unaware of what s/he is doing and could be open to change.

• The therapist is too friendly. This usually indicates that s/he is using therapy to meet her own needs rather than yours. If s/he seems to be spending too much time on a particular issue, talking too much about her/his own experience, or chatting socially for more than the first few minutes of the session, something is wrong. If s/he encourages intimate social contact between you outside of therapy, this is definitely inappropriate. Therapy is *not* friendship. If your therapist wants to pursue a friendship or sexual relationship with you, and your feelings are mutual, then you should terminate your contract as therapist and client.

• You and your therapist fight all the time. Therapists and clients do have occasional disagreements or arguments which need to be discussed and resolved. If you feel, however, that you and your therapist are engaged in a running battle that is never resolved, you could suggest enlisting the help of a third person to straighten things out, or you could explain how you feel and leave.

• Therapy makes you feel depressed, down on yourself, or discouraged. You feel you're in a rut with it, and it's going nowhere. Try to figure out with your therapist if there's some sort of resistance going on or if the therapist has not been attentive enough to your therapy. If nothing changes, this would be a good time to find another therapist.

• The therapist refuses to listen to feedback. You should be able to discuss doubts and criticisms in a non-defensive atmosphere. No one likes to be attacked, and most therapists are pretty sensitive if told that they aren't helping you, but you have a right to expect a therapist to listen to what you have to say. Do not tolerate being ignored or punished.

Termination

Termination is the ominous-sounding word for the last stage of the therapy process. For some women the end of this relationship is both exciting and satisfying; for others it is a time of ambivalence and uncertainty. How do you know when it is time to stop? How can you tell if your therapy has been successful?

There is no specific length of time that therapy should last. Short-term therapy, which focuses on one specific life crisis or one particular problem, usually lasts from three to nine months. Termination is relatively straightforward when you come to therapy with a certain goal, achieve it, and then leave. At the other extreme is psychoanalysis, which can consist of as much as five sessions a week for three to five years.

In the middle is long-term therapy. This applies to women who begin therapy with the need to tackle one problem and come to realize that this problem has roots which spread throughout the whole pattern of their lives. Often, too, women who enter long-term therapy enter with a vague, all-pervasive feeling of malaise which they cannot attribute to one specific problem. Long-term therapy can be as brief as one year or as long as or longer than five, but averages two to four years. Figuring out exactly where you fall in that considerable time spread is what makes termination difficult.

It is common at some midpoint in therapy to feel impatient and eager to finish. You may feel you are in a slump, nothing is happening, everyone else you know in therapy finished months before you. It is also common to feel terrified at the thought of leaving. When the subject of termination is raised, many women experience a recurrence of the same problems they came to therapy to solve.

Who decides when you are ready to terminate? You may hope that one day you and your therapist will simply look at each other and know it's time. This is rare. The decision is basically yours, and your therapist will probably wait for a cue from you that you are ready. If s/he disagrees with your decision, it is up to her/him to help you clarify the need you feel to terminate at that particular point and to clearly present why s/he feels your decision is premature. However, s/he should not try to force you into staying, just as s/he should not make any other decisions for you. If you are unable to reach an agreement with your therapist, it is a good idea to consult another therapist.

A therapist may suggest termination because s/he feels you will get no further benefit from the therapy. S/he may be in effect suggesting a different kind of therapy as more helpful (such as a group), or s/he may be suggesting that you try activities other than therapy for a while. You should inquire as to whether this decision is based on her/his assessment of your needs, or if it is made for personal reasons (e.g., change of schedule or financial problems).

The following are general guidelines to use when you are considering termination. They are not applicable to negative therapy relationships, which we discussed earlier in this chapter.

The woman who is ready to terminate therapy will probably feel a sense of control over her life because she has acquired the skills she needs in order to handle stress. Also, if she came to therapy without a support network of friends and people she can turn to, she has probably moved in the direction of creating this for herself.

Another indication of readiness to terminate is the ability of the client to see her therapist as s/he really is rather than in an idealized or exaggerated way. Unrealistic expectations or denial that the therapist is a real person with a life of her/his own gradually disappear because the client no longer needs to depend on therapy—she has essentially become her own therapist. Sessions become more friendly and chatty, maybe even boring. You don't need the "expert" anymore.

One situation which is neither ideal nor disastrous occurs when you feel you have been coasting in therapy so long that it becomes obvious you are not going to get any further. This may result from finally accepting the fact that therapy will not make you a perfect human being. This also happens when a therapist has unrealistic goals or expectations of her/his client.

You should never feel that the door is closed to further therapy. You may at some future point want to work on different issues, or you might experience a crisis in your life that requires extra support. If you are terminating therapy with good feelings about your therapist, ask whether or not s/he would be available for future emergencies or if you wanted to re-enter therapy.

Many clients (and therapists) wonder if it is possible to become friends after therapy has terminated. We feel that how clients and therapists relate to each other after the therapy contact is terminated is a private matter and not a professional concern. Therapists usually enjoy hearing from former clients, since they have a lot invested in a client's continued progress; but it will be up to you to initiate this contact.

NOTES

1. Edna Rawlings and Dianne Carter, "Feminist and Nonsexist Psychotherapy," *Psychotherapy for Women,* pp. 58–64.

Chapter 12

Common and Uncommon Complaints

Even the best of therapy relationships sometimes hits snags; but with a therapist you like and trust, most of these will be relatively minor. Problems can usually be resolved quickly if they are dealt with openly and not allowed to fester and develop into major grievances. Some complaints, however, are more serious and consequently raise more serious questions—questions such as what action is appropriate to take and where can help be found to deal with the problem. In either case, the sooner the problem is handled, the better. You will not get any help from a therapy relationship in which you feel uncomfortable or aggrieved in some way, and a good therapist will want to know what s/he is doing that bothers you.

Giving and Receiving Criticism or Feedback

The following discussion of the process of giving and receiving criticism can be helpful in individual therapy, in group therapy, or in other kinds of groups. Many support groups use what is known as a criticism/self-criticism model, reserving some time at the end of each meeting for discussion of the group process to insure that grievances are not suppressed for a long time. It is important, before attempting to use any criticism techniques, to make sure that you and your therapist (or others) are working toward the same goal (in therapy the goal will usually include helping you become a strong and independent person). If you do not feel your therapist is someone you basically trust and respect, then your problem is serious enough to consider not being in therapy with this person at all. If your therapist has your best interests at heart, s/he will want to hear what you feel is wrong.

My therapist solicited my reactions and sometimes was very receptive ("You're right, I'm sorry") and other times wasn't ("I think you have a problem accepting what I'm saying").

If you are planning to give feedback to your therapist, think about what you want to convey and perhaps practice it beforehand with someone else to make sure you are making your point clearly. Try to anticipate your therapist's reactions; therapists can be defensive, too, especially if you are raising questions about how they have handled a situation. Be prepared to discuss the situation; if you make unilateral demands for change (or for an apology), the therapy relationship becomes an adversary one. You must also be open to feedback or criticism from the therapist.

Here are some guidelines to keep in mind when you think about what you want to say to your therapist.[1] They can also be useful for groups to keep in mind for each session. Not each and every guideline will apply to every situation, but they will keep you on the road to constructive criticism.

• Be specific and concrete. Describe specific behavior

rather than making vague statements that are judgmental. If you say, "You are always late," or "You never listen to me," it is hard for a therapist to respond non-defensively. Instead, if you can say, "Last week you were late for our appointment; I felt I was unimportant to you because you didn't even tell me why you were late," this gives the therapist a specific incident to relate to, as well as some concrete information about your feelings.

If I think she's doing something I don't like, I just speak up. Sometimes it takes me a while, but I do get to it. This happened only once. My therapist made a comment once that she had learned not to count on my paying her regularly, since my finances were so shaky. I thought that was out of line and told her so. It was fine—there was no disagreement and the subject was dropped.

• Describe behavior as much as possible rather than evaluating it and labeling the other person. Don't say, "You're a bad therapist because . . . ," which is a loaded value judgment and bound to make the other person defensive. Instead, you can say, "Sometimes when I am talking, you interrupt me and I lose my train of thought. It makes it hard for me to talk about things I need to talk about here." Again, you have offered an example of some specific behavior in terms that can be discussed. Even when giving a compliment, it helps to be specific about what someone does that you like. Otherwise, they will not know what they should continue doing.

• Try to describe your feelings. Most of us have been alienated from our feelings to one degree or another, and women especially have been criticized for having "too many feelings." Therefore, many women have felt that they have to have strong, provable reasons before they can express dissatisfaction with another person. In fact, your feelings are important, and it is important to acknowledge them. The other person may not agree with your feelings, but this does not make them invalid. Sometimes people have learned to describe feelings but still attack the other person, e.g., "I feel you are a dumb person. That's my honest feeling." Obviously, that's not what we mean by describing feelings. You must have some confidence that the other person will accept your feelings and respond with her/his own. For example, you may say, "I feel very scared when I question you," instead of "You make me scared." You have to have some trust that the other person will reflect honestly on the issue and question her/his own actions rather than simply respond, "And why do you feel that way?" or "What is it about you that makes you respond that way?"

• It is important to bring criticisms forward as soon as possible after the incident that triggered them has taken place, even if it seems to be a minor criticism. If you save up criticisms or grievances and then spring them on your therapist all at once, don't be surprised to find a negative, unresponsive attitude. It may be hard for a therapist to remember clearly an incident that occurred three months or even a few weeks ago. If you have been brooding on it and going over it in your mind every day, details may stand out for you; but it is only natural that it may have receded into the past for your therapist. You haven't missed your chance if you didn't bring something up immediately, however; just try to relate past behavior to present behavior and try to understand that a therapist (or anyone else) can't always redress an injury done months or weeks back.

I'm very anxious and hesitant about giving feedback and as a result, I tend to postpone it until resentments have accumulated. My past therapists have responded defensively and my present therapist did once also. I would have liked them to be more accepting and objective instead of reacting as though I were attacking them or else ignoring it and acting as though it was inappropriate.

• When you have clarified what you are reacting to and how you are feeling about it, try to state what it is you want the other person to do about it. Again, this is not a situation in which you can demand a change; but the clearer that you can be about what it is you do want, the more likely it is that the other person can respond to the criticism. In groups it is important to be specific about *who* you want to change. Saying, "Some people ought to be more sensitive . . ." will let everyone off the hook ("She must mean someone else"). You have to be specific about who it is you think should change and in what way. It is also important to try to be concrete rather than abstract. "I want you to be nicer to me" is not helpful. "I would like you to look at me when I speak" is more specific in describing what you need. Also, try to own your feelings. For instance, "I feel such and such" rather than "We feel . . ." or "A lot of people feel. . . ."

• Try to explain why you want the other person to change; don't say, "A good therapist wouldn't treat me that way," but, "I need to be treated in this particular way in order to be helped." If you can explain what your specific needs are, it is more likely your therapist can try to meet them. If your approach is to punish other people or make them feel guilty about their behavior, they may change but it will not be a positive or long-lasting change. You must be able to explain why a particular change would be better for everyone in the long run.

• It is helpful to check feedback to insure that it has been understood. Ask the other person to paraphrase what you said to see if they got the point you were making. You can simply say, "Do you know what I mean?" and see if the other person understood your message.

• When you are receiving criticism, try to empathize with the person giving it and understand what they are saying instead of reacting defensively. You do not have to allow someone to dump on you, but listen to the description of their feeling and the way in which they want you to change. Paraphrase it back to them and see if they can now be less harsh. If the other person continues to name-call or make value judgments ("You're irresponsible," "You have no respect for my needs"), refuse to accept it. If you are offering feedback to your therapist, s/he should be able to take it in this style, i.e., be sensitive to what you are trying to say and participate in trying to help you state it in a useful manner. However, s/he is not there to be dumped on either.

If your therapist is not interested in feedback in the manner we have been talking about, you share no unity of purpose and you are in the wrong place. It is to be hoped that this criticism process is part of what should have been going on in good therapy, even without particular griev-ances. If it has been missing completely, the therapy is probably not going to be effective for you. Some common arguments against discussing the particulars of a griev-ance are: (1) it is less important than discussing your prob-lems or how you feel when you are angry, (2) you are avoiding looking at yourself and the changes you must make, (3) you are resisting by focusing on the therapist instead of yourself, (4) as the "expert" the therapist is in the best position to decide how to give therapy, set fees, handle clients, etc. Being aware of these difficulties and of the guidelines to support your feelings is not always enough to help you face your dilemma, and it is a painful realization to be disappointed by a therapist. After all, therapy was going to help end some difficulties, not start them.

Minor Complaints

The following are some minor problems which often come up in therapy. Many of them can be avoided if you and the therapist discuss them as part of the therapy contract and decide on a policy.

APPOINTMENT TIME SCHEDULES

You should agree with your therapist in the initial sessions about a time schedule for appointments: what time to meet, for how long, and what kind of notification each of you will give the other if an appointment has to be missed. If the therapist must miss an appointment, it should be planned in advance or you should be given an adequate explanation. It should be clear whether or not there is room in the therapist's schedule to change appointment times if necessary. If your schedule changes, or your therapist's does, you should try to work out a new meeting time as far in advance as possible. You should expect a therapist to try to make changes for you when your school or work schedule changes, but you cannot expect the therapist to work an additional night or ask other clients to give up their time for you.

One sore spot for clients is being asked to pay for appointments they miss. This may seem unfair if you are sick, have a sick child or are otherwise unavoidably detained. On the other hand, your therapist cannot schedule another client for the time reserved for you and, if you frequently miss appointments, has no way to replace the lost income. You and your therapist need to agree on a policy about missed appointments. You should be able to miss an appointment without paying if you give a week's notice, but you should understand that the therapist will want to be paid anywhere from the full fee to half the fee for an appointment that you cancel on the same day, for instance. Try to discuss what to do in case of illness and work out something that seems fair to both of you.

Vacation schedules present a similar difficulty. Some therapists insist that clients take vacations at the same time as they do; otherwise they expect to be paid for regular appointments during that time. We feel this is unreasonable, but also feel clients should give notice as soon as possible about any prolonged absence they plan (more than two weeks). A client cannot take a vacation of several months and expect to have a scheduled hour still reserved on her return unless some special arrangement has been made. Therapists should also let clients know as soon as possible about their vacation plans, especially if they take long vacations. Clients should know if the therapist can provide emergency coverage while they are away, or if the therapist can be reached in an emergency.

APPOINTMENT TIMES AND INTERRUPTIONS

Clients should be able to expect that a therapist will be on time for appointments. Most therapists schedule appointments for a standard amount of time (fifty minutes to one and one-half hours) and expect to begin and end on time. Sometimes it is unavoidable that they go over the time limit, but this should not be a frequent occurrence. If your therapist is consistently late because of earlier appointments, you should discuss a change of schedule.

You should also expect your time with the therapist to be uninterrupted. Occasionally there may be an emergency phone call or some other unavoidable interruption, but routinely the therapist should have an answering service or some other way of preventing interruptions. The therapy location is also important. Is it comfortable and reasonably sound-proofed? You can't feel comfortable and open if you can hear the people in the next room and feel they can hear you.

AVAILABILITY OUTSIDE APPOINTMENT TIMES

You and your therapist should set some policy in your contract about phone calls or appointments at times other than your regular time. You cannot expect your therapist to always have time to see you, but s/he should be available by phone to help determine the true extent of an emergency. You should expect your calls and messages to be answered within a day. Don't rely on leaving just one message for your therapist, feeling abandoned when your call is not answered. A message can get lost or be misunderstood, so call back. Therapists don't like middle-of-the-night calls any better than anyone else, but most therapists would rather be awakened at 2:00 A.M. than to find you in a hospital later in the morning. If your therapist brushes off phone calls no matter what the problem, or is never available, you have a real grievance.

Therapists in private practice are not always available for calls and may have little back-up. If you or your therapist anticipate problems, talk over what to do if the therapist can't be reached. In agencies or group practices, someone may be there to cover for the therapist, but you may not want to talk to that person. On the other hand, if it is a real emergency, you may be glad of the contact.

NOTE-TAKING OR RECORDING

The issue of what records are kept of therapy appointments is an important one (see Chapter 11). You have a right to see records that are being kept about you, whether by a private therapist or an agency. You also have a right to know what information is shared within an agency or in supervision.

A therapist's note-taking during a session, however, may be disturbing to you. Many therapists take some notes while talking with the client, but the notes should not be more important than the discussion itself, and the note-taking should not be intrusive. Don't get caught up in the idea that when a therapist starts to write, you have just said something important. Instead, ask your therapist about her/his note-taking habits and see if they can be modified to make you more comfortable. Therapists may often take notes at the beginning of therapy when you are presenting a lot of factual information that they would like to have for later reference.

CONTENT IN THERAPY SESSIONS

Sometimes both client and therapist use small talk at the beginning of the session as a way of warming up to each other when they meet. If it continues throughout a large part of the session, however, you have to decide if you or your therapist is perpetuating it. If you are avoiding something and your therapist is cooperating, something needs to change. You are not there to provide entertainment for each other; this time should be used for discussing your problems.

At the same time, your therapist may ask questions which seem irrelevant to you, but for which s/he has a purpose. S/he may want to get a better sense of your lifestyle or your typical reactions rather than indulge in an isolated discussion of problem areas. Your therapist is also establishing a relationship with you, and this is essentially the medium through which treatment takes place, unlike a medical situation wherein you describe symptoms and the doctor prescribes treatment. Solutions lie in understanding the whole of your life, not just the part that gives you trouble. If you don't understand why your therapist asked a particular question, find out why.

SHARING INFORMATION OR AVOIDING QUESTIONS

You should be able to expect your therapist to answer questions openly and honestly. Some therapists (especially analytically-oriented therapists) have a policy of not answering questions about anything of a personal nature. You should decide whether you wish to abide by these rules rather than entering into a long-term struggle over it, because such therapists are not likely to change, and you could spend months fruitlessly arguing about it. The analytical position, and one that has become traditional in many agencies, is that sharing any crumb of personal information dilutes the transference and makes it harder for the client to deal with her own issues. We feel that avoiding legitimate questions further mystifies the therapy relationship, making it an impersonal and dehumanizing experience.

Therapists should be willing to share information about credentials and training, philosophy of therapy, and fees and the basis for them. We also feel that therapists should be willing to share factual information about their own life situations when it is appropriate for the client to know. This includes such information as whether the therapist is married, single, divorced, living in a relationship, gay, or straight. Many therapists are willing to share such information and to use it in some way in the therapy by giving some examples from their own experience. Others do not like to discuss actual incidents from their lives. You should not expect your therapist to share intimate details of her/his life, since this time must be devoted to you and is not based on an even exchange of information.

SMOKING

Some therapists may ask you not to smoke while in a session. This is because smoking relieves tension and drains off anxiety, thus making it easier for you to avoid issues during the session. In addition, in therapies in which body movement is part of the treatment (such as bioenergetics), cigarettes present a clear danger.

You, as a client, may object to being subjected to a therapist's smoking, and you have a right to expect a therapist to be able to go for an hour without smoking.

In groups smoking often becomes a major issue, and discussion can go on for months with the smokers and non-smokers lined up against one another. Do not expect to enter a group wherein smoking is an established custom and have the rules changed. You will not win, and you will spend a lot of time in futile discussion.

SOCIAL INTERACTION

In the past many therapists had strict guidelines about socializing with their clients outside of the office, but if you happen to live in a small community it is not always possible to avoid meeting. If it is clear that there will be occasions when you and your therapist might meet socially, discuss how you both feel about it and how you should handle it. In large meetings or groups, it should pose no problem. In a smaller group, though, you may feel somewhat uncomfortable. In any case, you should be able to expect no one but your therapist to know what you two have talked about. You should also legitimately assume that you will not talk about therapy issues when you meet. This is time off for both of you. Remember that the assumption in most therapies is that intimate social involvement between client and therapist is not possible or desirable, since it changes the nature of the relationship for both.

CHANGE IN TECHNIQUE

At some point in your therapy the therapist may suggest a change in technique for you. This may be because s/he has just learned a new technique or because s/he thinks you have gone as far as you can with the present technique. In any case, discuss it thoroughly before you agree to the change. You should not have to make up your mind until a later session, once you have had time to think it over.

Most of the above grievances are minor unless ignored. If not handled, however, bad feelings can build up and lead to real anger. Clients as well as therapists have a right to set their priorities for the relationship, and it is better if this can be done as soon as the issues come up or at the outset of the relationship. You may not realize at the beginning of therapy precisely what will bother you, however, so you may not be able to bring it up at that time. Therapists, who have had more experience, will probably be more assertive about setting limits on such issues as appointment times, fees, or phone calls. These things are not irrevocable or unchangeable, though, and you have a right to suggest changes later on. You may have more trouble with these issues in an agency, where some policies are immutably set by the agency, and not by the therapist. However, if a therapist says that something is against agency policy, and it is really important to you (your right to see your records, for example), do not argue with the individual therapist (who may be unable to change the rules), but decide where else in the agency to deal with the problem.

Major Complaints

Major grievances are problems which are considerably more serious and may not be easily resolved if, indeed, they can be resolved at all. They may call for your leaving a therapist, reporting her/him to the appropriate agencies, or taking legal action. You may need to ask for the support and/or intervention of others to take any of these steps.

SEXUAL SEDUCTION

The most common major problem that women clients have had to deal with is inappropriate sexual behavior on the part of therapists, ranging from hugs or pats to sexual intercourse. These acts almost always take place between older male therapists and younger female patients, repeating patterns apparent in the rest of society. Such inappropriate behavior is not limited to these age groups, however, and may even take place between same-sex client and therapist. Some therapists have tried to justify sexual contact between therapist and client as necessary and therapeutic. The usual patterns of such contact, however, make it apparent that the sex meets the needs of the therapist and not those of the client. The justifications of therapists have been: the patient needed the sexual contact to make her less frigid; the patient was extremely seductive, and the therapist was complying with her needs; sex was a mutual need and agreed on between them; the therapist was in love with the patient, and so on. None of these rationalizations holds up under scrutiny.

I try to handle feedback directly, but sometimes that's hard. With the man I saw, I should have sued him (for sexual seduction). Instead, I wrote him a letter a year after I ended therapy—I couldn't sue, the issues were too hard for me.

No reputable school of therapy advocates sexual intimacy as a form of treatment, and most specifically forbid it. In the case of the claim that a client has been seductive, the therapist is still in charge of the situation and should be expected to handle it appropriately. Therapists know that in many therapy relationships strong feelings on the part of the client toward the therapist arise, and are referred to as transference. They may be positive or negative feelings, but in any case must be handled as part of the therapy process, not acted out. If the therapist and client agree that their attraction is mutual and wish to follow through on it, therapy should be terminated before a social relationship is initiated. This might still be a questionable situation, depending on the motivation of both client and therapist to become sexually involved, but at least they would be removing their relationship from the guise of therapy.

The male therapist I saw decided that what I "needed" was to have sex with him. In hindsight, I feel that I got totally ripped off —in my vulnerability at that time for me. Male therapists are difficult for me to relate to unless I have a real clear view of them and their intentions.

When you are not in the situation, it may be hard to understand how it could arise and how a woman could be taken advantage of in this way. It is important to realize that when you go into therapy, you may be in an emotionally vulnerable state, feeling upset, self-critical, lonely, or in need of love. Feelings like these can cause you to reach out to your therapist for love or to respond to overtures made by the therapist. The therapist is in a position of some authority and power. The woman may have trouble resisting what an authority figure says is good for her; or she may feel that if she turns him down, her therapist will refuse to see her any longer. She is especially vulnerable if she has had a hard time finding a therapist and fears losing this one.

It has been difficult for women to report such problems or decide what to do about them. If you encounter difficulties with a private practitioner, there may be no immediately apparent authority or agency to whom to report such conduct. In an agency, feelings about not wanting to hurt the therapist may prevent you from reporting him. And, in fact, many women who have tried to report such behavior have met with disbelief or have had the accusation turned against them. Until more and more women began to speak out and it became impossible to ignore them, the prevailing Freudian theory was that women who reported sexual encounters with their therapist were fantasizing the relationship because they desired it so strongly.

In more ambiguous situations, some women have been unsure that they were actually propositioned and hesitated to take action unless they were sure. If the overtures have been simply hugs or playful touches, you may believe the good intent of your therapist; but if you feel uncomfortable, it is your right to demand that such behavior stop and that you not be subjected to pejorative remarks because of your discomfort (e.g., being told you are frigid, scared, not a real woman, etc.). These "little rapes" are often a problem in less conventional therapies wherein the client (or group) is using various action methods. While touching and hugging are common and often legitimate in these situations, there should be no expectation on the part of the therapist or other clients that anyone allow herself to be used against her will.

I used to have a male counselor who would tell me I was castrating him when I reacted negatively to anything he said, who played games with me to see how I'd react and who gave me more problems than I had when I came in. Now I can see he was wrong, not me.

It may be difficult to believe that this could happen to you, but it has happened to many women who were not weak, psychotic, or stupid. For good accounts of sexual seduction in therapy, read *Betrayal* by Julie Roy and Lucy Freeman, *Women and Madness* (Chapter 5) by Phyllis Chesler, and *Shrinks, etc.* (Chapter 1) by Thomas Kiernan.[2] Julie Roy's work is especially important because she successfully sued a prestigious and well-credentialed psychoanalyst for seduction, and won.

PREJUDICE AGAINST HOMOSEXUALITY

If you are a lesbian or bisexual, and your therapist believes that homosexuality is a disease, then you are faced with a major problem in therapy. You may find that your therapist is trying to "cure" you against your will and that s/he is interpreting every problem you report as a symptom of your "deviant" sexuality. You may encounter a total lack of understanding of many of your feelings.

Many therapists absorbed prejudice against unconventional sexual preference with their training. It is still commonly presumed that people who choose same-sex partners are seriously disturbed and, furthermore, that they are unhappy about their sexual choice. This notion has become firmly established in the minds of many therapists who have worked with homosexuals who *were* unhappy about their sexual preference and/or lifestyle. The reasons for that unhappiness, however, might never be fully explored—e.g., feeling totally isolated from a normal social life, being forced to be secretive or else open to ridicule or worse, or feeling lack of any community of support.

Many lesbians have reported that when they seek to undergo therapy, their lesbianism is presumed to be the problem, and the issues for which they sought help are ignored while the therapist focuses on their sexual preference. For example, many women who went into therapy to work on the depression they felt about not being able to be open with their families about their lives were told that they would simply have to change their lifestyle. Even if this is not the case, lesbians may find it difficult to get help in achieving a positive self-image from a therapist who is unable to believe that homosexuality can be a healthy and positive lifestyle for some people.

Recently, lesbians, gay men, and others concerned about human rights have advocated the acceptance of homosexuality as a choice and right like any other. There has been much controversy in psychiatric circles about the decision to change the diagnostic classification of homosexuality to "Sexual Orientation Disturbance" and a later decision to ignore it completely as a diagnostic category. This controversy will undoubtedly continue for many years. It is important for women to understand that this is a moral issue and not a medical or scientific one. No therapist has the right to impose social values or prejudice in the guise of treatment.

IATROGENIC DISEASES

The term *iatrogenic* describes problems caused by treatment for another disease, such as a doctor leaving a sponge inside the patient during an operation. Even if the operation was a success, the patient is in trouble. In psychiatric situations, it is difficult to prove that your problems were exacerbated as a result of going to a therapist, or that you wouldn't have had certain problems if you had never been in therapy; but there are still areas in which legitimate doubts can be raised. Most of these involve the use of drugs, shock treatment, psychosurgery, or illegal detention or hospitalization. Many doctors and hospital staff, for example, have been used to operating by fiat and have not seriously considered the legal rights of their patients. Recent years have seen an upsurge in malpractice suits against such doctors, serving notice that women are becoming more aware that they have a right to challenge the hitherto unchallenged practice of doctors.

You should be aware of your right to informed consent. Before any procedure can be undertaken, you must give written consent, unless you are an involuntary (committed) patient. You have the right to a full explanation of the procedure and to the opinion of a second doctor. If medication is prescribed, you have the right to know what it is and what the possible side effects are. Many doctors withhold such information from patients on the grounds that the knowledge would encourage them to imagine they are suffering from these side effects. We believe this is not the doctor's choice to make. You should familiarize yourself with the possible side effects of any drug prescribed to you. If a psychiatrist wants to hospitalize you against your will, you have the right to consult a lawyer.

If you feel you are suffering new problems as a direct result of therapy (particularly drug therapy), discuss your feelings with your therapist. If her/his response is unsatisfactory, you should consult another therapist.

Notes

1. Gracie Lyons, *Constructive Criticism.*

2. Lucy Freeman and Julie Roy, *Betrayal;* Phyllis Chesler, *Women and Madness;* Thomas Kiernan, *Shrinks, etc.*

Chapter 13

Hospitalization

If you assume this chapter has nothing to do with you, you are wrong. If you are considering seeing a therapist, if you are currently in therapy, if a friend or relative thinks you should be in therapy, this chapter could be very important to you. Statistics show that at some point in her/his lifetime, one out of every ten Americans will be hospitalized for "mental illness." So it is altogether possible that you, a friend, or a relative may be hospitalized at some time. There is additional evidence that more women than men are psychiatrically hospitalized in this country, and that the numbers of women being hospitalized are increasing.

Some people become so incapacitated by their own feelings that they are unable to cope with day-to-day problems or take any responsibility for themselves. Some are the victims of physical problems which severely affect their minds. These people need asylum in the true sense of the word—a place to be safe. Yet today's mental hospital does not provide the sheltered environment people need in order to recover from severe emotional trauma. The majority of people in psychiatric hospitals need not be there, or would at least be far better off in a more therapeutic environment.

I had a breakdown in college six years before I began therapy. I was hospitalized for one week and given sleeping pills frequently. I thought I was insane and finally a friend encouraged me to leave the hospital. I think hospitalization was a bad solution to my problem, but I don't know what the consequences would have been from not going at all or receiving other treatment. How can I compare? It just happened. What I really wanted was someone to talk to right then and there. Since no one was available, they gave me a "sleep cure." I sleep a lot when I'm in a depressed state, but I don't use any drugs.

The "Catch 22" of being a mental patient is trying to talk to people who believe you are insane. Whatever you say probably won't be believed, and whatever you do will be interpreted as a symptom of your "illness." Most patients quickly learn what standard of behavior is acceptable to the staff and recognize that the only way to gain release is by conforming to that.

All mental patients, women and men, are oppressed by being labeled mentally ill. Women patients are doubly oppressed, but this perspective cannot be used to negate the experience of oppression that may be felt by male patients. We are not experts—in the sense that we have never been mental patients. Both of us have worked in mental hospitals and have been appalled at the dehumanization of the patients, but we realize that we cannot speak for the patients themselves. Our comments on hospitalization therefore come from our own perspective as therapists and feminists.

Why Are Women Hospitalized?

Many women are hospitalized because resources in the community are not adequate to meet their particular needs. Problems which might be minor are neglected until they are insurmountable and a woman or her family feel there is no alternative to hospitalization. Many women are hospitalized because they persist in behavior that is not regarded as compatible with their particular role. For instance, they may neglect to do their housework or make themselves attractive, may not want to devote themselves to their children, or may want sexual involvement with other women. Depression, alcoholism, drug abuse, and nervous breakdowns (the inability to cope with day-to-day living) are the most common reasons why women are hospitalized.

One problem which often leads to hospitalization is the *empty nest syndrome.*[1] This afflicts middle-aged women who, having spent most of their productive years at home rearing children, feel they no longer have any usefulness once the children grow up and leave home. This feeling of despair can be aggravated when the woman does not feel sexually attractive (especially if her husband has left her for a younger woman) or if she attempts to find employment outside the home and is rejected. Women like this are often treated by psychiatrists or family doctors with tranquilizers, barbiturates, and amphetamines—dangerous by themselves, but often deadly in any combination. In 1977, 57 million prescriptions were written for Valium, 15 million for Librium, 8 million for phenobarbital, and 9.7 million for meprobamate (Equanil, Miltown, or Solacen). Two thirds of these prescriptions were written for women.[2] It is easy for women to get into the wake-up pill in the morning, sleeping pill at night habit. Since the effect of these drugs is enhanced when taken in combination with alcohol, their use can easily lead to accidental or intentional overdoses, and then hospitalization.

Other women end up being hospitalized because of sexual acting out that is disapproved by society. Young women may be threatened with punishment, including hospitalization, because their standards of sexual behavior differ from those of their parents. Their behavior may not be against the law and may not be punishable through the court system, but it can often be manipulated into a hospital stay. The exploration of feelings about lesbianism may be characterized as sexual acting out, for instance; and young women who do so are often hospitalized by their parents, with the cooperation of a psychiatrist. Any woman under legal age can be signed into a hospital by parents who disagree with her on anything, ranging from her politics to her morals. For example, a young woman, active in the anti-war movement and involved in a relationship with a young man, was repeatedly locked in her room by her disapproving parents. When she tried to escape, she was committed to a private hospital on the grounds that she was out of control, promiscuous, and a repeated truant from school—her truancy the result only of her being restrained by her parents! Because she understandably did not want to be hospitalized and refused to cooperate with the staff, she was characterized as acting out, obstreperous, rebellious, and having problems with authority.

Because rape has been relegated to the criminal courts, and because the rape victim has been forced by the legal system to prove that an actual crime was committed, women have sometimes ended up in mental hospitals in the aftermath of a rape. A woman may become immobilized with fear and unable to function. Because adequate support in the community for rape victims has been lacking, and because they have so often been accused of seduction and provocation, dealing with the prosecution of a rape or even the reporting of it has often been as traumatic as the rape itself and has felt to some women like a repetition of the experience itself.

In recent years a number of women's services for rape victims have come into being, and in some cities, there is rape counseling or a rape crisis center. In other areas police and/or hospital employees have had special training to help them be more sensitive to the issues involved when a woman is raped. But these services have touched only the tip of the iceberg. In many places such services are not available or, if they are, they are not utilized by women. The old attitude that "she was asking for it" may yet prevail in hospitals and police stations. The particular burden of the thought "if only I had known what to do, it wouldn't have happened" is an extension of the double bind women are always in about their sexuality. The belief that it is somehow a woman's fault that she has been raped is victim-blaming at its worst.

Types of Mental Hospitals

Whether or not you expect to be hospitalized, you probably have your own fantasies about mental hospitals and mental patients. One common fantasy about mental patients is that they are prone to violence. In fact, they tend to exhibit less violence than do people in a normal population. Another fantasy is that you can easily spot a mental patient. On the contrary, they are often not readily distinguishable from the doctors, nurses, orderlies and other hospital personnel. In some hospitals the staff is very possessive of the special clothing or symbols they wear or carry (such as white jackets or keys) because they are the only visible signs distinguishing them from the patient population. In other hospitals, it is not necessary to wear badges of distinction, since the patients are routinely denied their own clothing and wear the hospital "uniform" of pajamas and robe. Your fantasy of the hospital may not be of a "snake pit," but rather of a restful sojourn away from the everyday cares of the world. Some women feel that the hospital will be a panacea, an isolated place to get away from it all, to resolve their problems, and to seek out wise and omniscient medical counsel. They have visions of taking long walks in the gardens, having daily consultation with a kindly but strong doctor, eating meals served by a gracious staff, and, above all, enjoying freedom from their usual routine. In fact, the quiet which may prevail is due to the fact that almost every patient in a mental hospital (private or public) receives tranquilizing medication. No matter what hospital you enter, a preponderance of patients will be heavily drugged, and many will be exhibiting some of the symptoms which psychotropic drugs can induce.

In reality hospitals offer an astounding range of treatment and staffing patterns. Older state hospitals often do come close to the "snake pit" image because of their deteriorating facilities and inadequate staff. The lack of sufficient funds for indigent patients means that they must do without many basic amenities. Patients may not have appropriate clothing and, as the fiscal year draws to a close, medication may be cut back drastically until the next year's budget is available. Because such hospitals were built far from the cities, visiting them is difficult. They are also huge, sometimes built to house 5,000 or more patients. They are like self-contained villages, and for patients who have been there many years, the world outside can be a frightening place.

While all patients face the stigma of being mental patients and therefore of being viewed as untrustworthy, the poor and Third World women may face an additional stigma of being characterized in certain ways because of their race and class. For example, poor women may not have anyone to bring them their own clothes while they are on the ward, and may therefore look "sicker" simply because they are dressed in ill-fitting hospital garments. Often patients are treated like animals without human intelligence—sometimes in a kindly way, sometimes brutally, but always without that important human connection. Differences of treatment based on racial prejudice are manifest in the fact that Black people (especially men) are more likely to be put in seclusion or involuntarily medicated if they use aggressive language. The hospital staff seems to feel that there is a greater potential for violence in Blacks than in whites.

The old state hospitals may seem outmoded now, but they still house large numbers of patients. Teaching hospitals (attached to universities) often have better facilities and larger staffs, are more conveniently located for visits both to and from family, and seem to offer better treatment. One drawback of teaching hospitals, however, is that some staff, particularly resident psychiatrists, move on to other wards at intervals of from three months to a year. So if your schedule of illness doesn't match their rotation, you have to make the adjustment to a new therapist. The multiplicity of services may be confusing and, despite the team approach of many hospitals, the patient may be pulled in several directions at once by competing staff. This is especially true for "interesting" patients, usually portrayed as young, attractive, verbal, intelligent, and sophisticated women. These patients may get lots of attention, be considered candidates for individual therapy, or be placed in special programs, while other patients are ignored. Middle-aged or post-menopausal women are often regarded as boring, demanding, not worth the time and energy of the staff, and are often fobbed off with medication while their problems are dismissed as trivial or unreal. An additional problem in teaching hospitals is the fact that patients may be selected for treatment on the basis of on-going research projects. There may be less consideration of the patient's needs than of the hospital program (e.g., one week they may be admitting schizophrenics under the age of thirty, the next week it may be manic-depressives with a history of some special complaint).

In the hospital, women are often pushed to conform to traditional gender roles of wife, mother, and nurturer and are rewarded for showing "feminine" behavior like putting on makeup or asking to go to the beauty shop. They may be punished (by having privileges taken away) for "non-feminine" behavior such as arguing, not wanting to go home to visit family, or not wanting to perform the tasks of a housewife. In many mental hospitals women are offered access to cooking or sewing groups while men are offered shop or woodworking.

A woman who was hospitalized eight times within a few years related that most of her "therapy" consisted of different combinations of drugs. She said of one state hospital experience, "The conditions in the state hospital are appalling and I would say from what I've read and heard that it is a better place than usual. I received no private therapy while there but two very pretty women, one who came in after I did, received one-to-one therapy. My doctor told me I needed it and would get it, but Diane won—she was much prettier."

There are also many private mental hospitals to which patients may be admitted by the psychiatrist with whom they are in therapy. Once admitted, the patient may be visited by her own doctor, or her treatment may be in the hands of the staff. Although she might expect daily visits from her doctor, she would be surprised to find that these last for only a few minutes, scarcely time to say hello, let alone undergo therapy. Some private hospitals are referred to as shock shops because almost every patient who is admitted is given shock treatment. Other private hospitals may offer a full range of services from analytic psychotherapy to occupational and recreational therapy, but the costs are exorbitant, and the length of the patient's stay may be determined not by need but by the amount of insurance coverage available to her.

What have all these hospitals in common? None of the patients have control over their own lives. The more expensive private hospitals may give the patient the illusion of control, but underneath the message is the same: "You are crazy and the staff knows what's best for you." In the chronic wards of the state hospitals, patients have none of the things we take for granted—the right to privacy in the bathroom, the right to take a shower more than once a week, or the right to make a phone call. In more plush hospitals patients may have private rooms, good food, reading material, their own clothes to wear, or spending money; but should the patient attempt to do something that has been forbidden by the doctor or by hospital policy (e.g., not getting up in the morning, not wearing shoes on the ward, or not combing her hair), she will quickly find out that the feeling of choice and control is an illusion.

How Do You Get In?

VOLUNTARY ADMISSION

Most hospital admissions are *voluntary,* but that word has little to do with actual willingness or a desire to be in a hospital. Some people are voluntary patients because they sought out hospitalization, because they consulted a therapist who recommended hospitalization, or because a friend or relative took them to a hospital during a crisis. They may have decided to sign voluntary admission papers because they were told they could sign out any time they wanted, because they were told they would be committed if they didn't sign in voluntarily, or because family or friends refused to take them home again.

Informed consent is the serious issue in question here. Does the patient really know what is happening and what the alternatives are? Does she understand the constraints? For example, rather than allowing a patient to leave at will, most states require that voluntary patients desiring to leave the hospital file a written request on the correct forms (which must be obtained from someone on the nursing staff) and then wait some period of time (up to several days) before they are released. This gives the hospital time to commit the patient through court action if they so desire.

What else is the patient consenting to by signing into the hospital? A recent court case (Rogers v. Okin) in the United States District Court of Massachusetts against Boston State Hospital asserts the right of hospitalized patients to refuse medication or other treatment without being penalized, unless there is an emergency situation. Previously it had been assumed that patients in the hospital must submit to any treatment prescribed by the doctor (with the exception of shock treatment or psychosurgery, for which additional, signed consent is needed). This means that if, for example, a patient refuses medication in pill form, it could be forcibly given as a liquid or by injection.

INVOLUNTARY ADMISSION

Patients who are *involuntary* or *committed* enter hospitals through a variety of procedures which vary from state to state. In some states it is enough for one physician (whom you may not know or trust) to sign papers asking that you be hospitalized for observation; in other states it may require two physicians, or a petition may be made by a psychologist or by a relative. A relative who has obtained a petition asking that you be hospitalized for observation may call the police to have you taken to a hospital. In almost any state, if you are a minor, your parents can sign you into the hospital. Often the police have discretionary powers, which means that if they arrest you on any other charge, but feel your behavior to be peculiar, they can arrange to have you interviewed by a court psychiatrist and hospitalized for observation.

Once you are under observation in a hospital, a court review of your case must take place within a specified time (from five to ten working days), at which time you will be either released or committed. You might be offered the choice at that point of signing voluntary papers rather than being committed. Often the court proceedings are held in hospital buildings themselves, and patients are brought in wearing hospital pajamas and robes. There may be a lawyer appointed to you; but should you be challenging your commitment, you will not have had time to meet with this lawyer nor to discuss what course you want followed. As in most other situations, patients often find that they lack credibility merely as a result of being a patient—the very condition they may be disputing. Each state has different regulations about how commitment proceedings are handled. Find out what they are in your state before you need to know.

When it comes to admission to a hospital and especially when it comes to commitment by a court, you may have the impression that there is some objective standard of mental disturbance that you are being measured against. This is not the case. Overburdened courts pay more attention to the professionals (doctors and social workers) who are testifying about your needs than they do to you. In their turn, professionals and courts alike tend to give more weight to the testimony of relatives than to the testimony of the patient—after all, you're in and they're out, a fact that makes your word automatically suspect. This can clearly work to your disadvantage when you have come to a hospital during an emotional crisis or after having taken an overdose of medication. You may be confused and unable to remember some details of your crisis. This will be duly noted by the authorities and can be used as evidence of your "condition."

The ability of doctors to adequately diagnose anyone seeking admission to a mental hospital has been severely questioned. In a study conducted by D. L. Rosenhan[3] volunteers with no history of psychiatric problems sought admission to several hospitals, falsifying nothing about themselves except for stating that they each heard a hollow voice which said "thud." None had any difficulty being admitted to a hospital; but furthermore, none was identified during their stay as being normal, despite the fact that the initial "symptom" disappeared immediately upon admission. Thus, the standards by which one is judged sane are very loose indeed.

Despite the problem of people being hospitalized when they don't want to be, there is also the opposite problem of people who request hospitalization and are turned away. This may seem contradictory after seeing how easily the Rosenhan "patients" were admitted; but in fact, this contradiction does exist. Often patients do not really need to be confined because they are not dangerous to themselves or others, but they have been brought to the hospital because there are few or no other resources for treatment in the community. The decision about admission may be totally arbitrary, depending, for instance, on who is on duty on a particular day. Often, relatives requesting that a patient be hospitalized are refused because the patient may not meet the hospital's definition of a patient or show the same behavior to the doctor that she showed at home; because the hospital might be too crowded or taking only patients from certain geographical locations or with certain kinds of problems.

How Do You Get Out?

When patients have been committed for observation, there is usually a designated time period during which they must be seen by the court; after that court proceeding, if they are committed to the hospital, the commitment is indefinite. Various states have various rules about a review of the records after a length of time, but overworked bureaucracies often give perfunctory reviews, and there are many horror stories about patients who have remained in the system for years until they no longer even wanted to leave or had anyplace else to go.

Voluntary patients are dependent primarily on their doctors for release. What the doctor's criteria are for diagnosing a cure could range anywhere from a reasonable assessment of your ability to cope with your problems or a depletion of your insurance funds, to a recommendation from the hospital staff. In mental hospitals, in order to earn staff agreement to and support for your release, you may have to hide your true feelings and let the staff hear what they want to hear. It is possible for you to petition to be released "against advice," but you may be in some danger of being committed if your doctor feels you are not in control of your behavior.

Although many patients find it difficult to gain release from the hospital, under certain arbitrary conditions release becomes easy. When hospitals are overcrowded and funds are short, the staff may be happy to help people leave the hospital; but they may not have time or interest to see that the appropriate steps are taken. If you have friends or relatives outside the hospital who are willing to help, they are your best bet for getting out. Hospitals like to know that you have a place to go when you leave and to know that you have made some plans for what you will do on your release. Some hospitals have half-way houses or day-hospital programs that act as a bridge to the community. You can ask about these programs and try to use their resources to speed you on your way.

Patient and ex-patient activist groups exist in many states. For example, in Massachusetts, the Mental Patients Liberation Front distributes a handbook of patients' legal rights (see Appendix B) and also sponsors meetings on some hospital wards. Groups like these can be a valuable aid in your transition to community life since they do not require that you stifle your feelings about your hospital stay.

Alternatives to Hospitalization

Unfortunately, today there are few alternatives to hospitalization. People who are hospitalized are often not regarded highly enough to warrant the expenditure of time and energy necessary to build alternatives. In other situations, when a community mental health service is seen as a viable alternative, it has become a political football providing jobs for mental health professionals rather than services for mental patients. In most cases, professionals have been the ones making the decisions about crucial programs, not patients themselves.

DAY HOSPITALS

Some of the alternatives to hospitalization which do exist provide the same kind of professionally-controlled environments that hospitals provide. These include day hospitals or day-treatment programs which clients visit every day, but which do not offer overnight accommodations. The idea is to provide a structured environment with scheduled activities such as therapy groups and occupational therapy, as well as some unscheduled time in which to simply relate to others. A positive aspect of this program is that it can help the client reestablish networks of friends that have been disturbed or broken by long stays in the hospital; it can also avoid the disruption of family networks by avoiding hospitalization altogether, allowing the client to go home every evening; and it avoids some of the stigma of being an in-patient. The drawbacks are that this program is, after all, run by the same people who run hospitals, and it fosters the same attitude about clients, even though that attitude may be better hidden. If the program takes place in a hospital rather than in a neighborhood facility, all of the problems of hospitalization may be present (e.g., long distance from home, stigma of hospitalization, lack of connection to neighborhood, or breaking down of social networks).

HALF-WAY HOUSES

Another alternative can sometimes be found in half-way houses. These facilities are usually residences for people on the way out of the hospital, as a way of helping them adjust to the community (or as a way of remaining permanently in a somewhat sheltered environment within the community). They can be a resource for the woman who does not want to enter a hospital but feels she needs a supportive environment.

Again, the kind of facilities available vary from state to state, and widely different institutions may be called halfway houses. Some are merely hotel-like residences with single rooms and additional rules and staff, providing meals and doling out medication. In other areas they may consist of cooperative apartments in which ex-patients share living space with students and staff and participate in preparing meals, cleaning up, or food shopping. The quality of the half-way house is totally dependent on the funds available to support it, and they are often in terrible disrepair and grossly understaffed.

PATIENT-CONTROLLED ALTERNATIVES

In her book *On Our Own*[4] Judi Chamberlin suggests an entirely different way of looking at alternatives to hospitalization. By offering models in which the alternative institution may be entirely controlled by patients or ex-patients, she is introducing a positive new element into the traditional picture of hospital inmates as a perpetual drag on society. Chamberlin's book cites a working alternative to the hospital system, showing that it is not just a pipe dream. This system also takes cognizance, for the first time, of the input that the consumers of a system ought to have into that system.

Because patients have been labeled crazy, little weight has been given to their statements about their own needs. Chamberlin has been a patient herself, though, and knows what many of the needs are, suggesting positive ways they can be dealt with. One example she cites is in a program in Vancouver (Vancouver Emotional Emergency Center), where patients are able to stay in a cooperative residence on an emergency basis. One room in the basement of this house is lined with mattresses and reserved for staff or residents to scream in when their feelings get out of hand. This alternative has almost never been suggested in more traditional programs; instead, patients have been expected to control their behavior and not act out by talking loudly, screaming, or acting violently. These traditional programs have ignored the fact that people who are allowed to express some of their feelings through screaming may be able to control themselves more acceptably in other situations. Since Elizabeth Kubler-Ross (the well-known authority on death and dying) has recently advocated screaming rooms in hospitals for both the bereaved and the staff who work with dying patients, they will probably become acceptable and more common.

Another alternative to the traditional mental health system is the patient-controlled groups known in different areas of the country by such names as Mental Patients' Liberation Front (Boston), Network Against Psychiatric Assault (San Francisco), or Network Against Psychiatric Oppression (New York). Most of these alternatives are still too small to offer more than support groups for patients and ex-patients. They do not have the clout at this time to offer ongoing programs and alternative services. In the meantime, they do offer a network of friends and helpers who have been in the hospital, who can help you stay out, and who welcome your participation at groups. They offer uncritical support, a tremendous amount of information, and a good place to develop and refine a political analysis of the plight of the mental patient. Most of these groups accept only patients and ex-patients as members, although they may have the support of professionals in the mental health field. Because of a commitment to patient-controlled alternatives, they may not have much to do with more traditional groups in an area. But they can be invaluable sources of information in helping obtain records from hospitals and overcoming other obstacles ex-patients may face.

The Elizabeth Stone House in Boston is an example of a feminist alternative to hospitalization. Like many under-financed alternatives to the traditional system, however, it has been fraught with difficulties. The house originally tried to offer a short-term refuge—a two-week stay as an alternative to hospitalization. At the same time, attempts were made to develop a longer-term residential program consisting of six people in a separate space making a com-mitment to living together for at least six months to a year. Both of these programs have had problems off and on be-cause of the tremendous energy required for this kind of work, because they have vacillated between volunteer and paid help, because the kinds and levels of financial sup-port have varied, and because of other difficulties. A full explanation of the experience of the House is far too in-volved to go into here, but it has been an experiment in-volving the input of patients and ex-patients, volunteers, and professionals. One of the advantages of this program is that it addresses problems never raised before, that is, the particular oppression of women in the psychiatric sys-tem and the difficulty of getting out of that system once you are in it. That such a program can receive funds from traditional sources but remain in control of its own inter-nal system also signifies a new approach to the mental health system.

This chapter barely scratches the surface of the prob-lem of mental hospitalization. Like most human services, this area is of a very low priority in the United States. More public pressure, additional funds, and greater recognition of the real needs of people in emotional distress might begin to have some impact on this colossal mess. Just as we turn our backs on our prison system, though, it seems we don't want to deal with mental hospitalization if we don't have to. Where we are beginning to see a change in this head-in-the-sand attitude is in the greater numbers of women dedicating themselves collectively to improving the quality of life for themselves and for all women, as well as in the greater collective voice of patients and ex-patients themselves.

Recommended Readings on Hospitalization

Many fictional accounts of mental hospitals paint a particularly vivid and realistic picture of life in a hospital. Although some details may not ring true, they are often more evocative of the hospital experience than are descriptive non-fiction accounts. We recommend *Woman on the Edge of Time* by Marge Piercy and *The Cracker Factory* by Joyce Rebeta-Burditt.

Accounts of patients' experiences and of patient-controlled alternatives are particularly useful for women looking for support. Factual accounts we recommend are *Too Much Anger, Too Many Tears* by Janet and Paul Gotkin and *Women Look at Psychiatry* edited by Dorothy Smith and Sara David. Resources for patient-controlled alternatives are *On Our Own: Patient-Controlled Alternatives to the Mental Health System* by Judi Chamberlin and *Your Rights as a Mental Patient in Massachusetts* by the Mental Patients Liberation Front. Newspapers which report on alternatives to the mental health system are *Madness Network News* (P.O. Box 684, San Francisco, Cal., 94101) and *State and Mind* (P.O. Box 89, West Somerville, Mass., 02144).

NOTES

1. Pauline Bart, "Depression in Middle-Aged Women," *Women in Sexist Society,* Gornick and Moran, eds., pp. 99–117.

2. Edward Edelson, "Women and Addiction," *Family Circle,* 10/23/78, p. 32.

3. D. L. Rosenhan, "On Being Sane in Insane Places," *Science,* Vol. 179, 1973.

4. Judi Chamberlin, *On Our Own: Patient-Controlled Alternatives to the Mental Health System.*

Appendix A

How to Locate a Therapist

All of the different information about kinds of therapy and therapists can compound the problem of finding a therapist when you don't know where to look. In a large urban area there is a bewildering array of mental health services available, and the problem becomes one of choosing which will meet your needs. In a small town or rural area, just locating a mental health service may be a problem, and there may not be many choices within your financial limits.

Referral Sources

TELEPHONE DIRECTORY. You can find specific services by checking in the white pages of the phone book or in the *Yellow Pages* under Social Services, Psychologists, or Psychotherapists. This is a good place to start if you know that you want a particular kind of service (e.g., family therapy, marriage therapy, etc.) or if you qualify for a particular agency (e.g., Veterans Administration).

REFERRAL AGENCIES. If you are looking for an individual therapist for yourself or for a private therapist for couples counseling, you might start with a service that is set up to give referrals. Commonly, you would be directed to the Medical Association or Mental Health Association in your locale for a referral. These are usually the worst places to start unless you have no other resources. They do not make personal recommendations but supply a list of names and are apt to recommend only medical practitioners or clinics. Beware, also, of "matchmaker" services who refer only within one specialty (like psychoanalysis) and who charge a high fee for referral work which other agencies could do for less money.

COUNSELING CENTERS. Other places which make referrals are hotlines or crisis counseling services. They usually do short-term drop-in or telephone counseling and will refer clients to others for long-term counseling or for a specific kind of counseling. Some agencies keep large referral lists and will spend several sessions with a client determining her needs and who could best help her. Often you will have to do the work of contacting the suggested referral, however, and you may be disappointed if things don't work out for one reason or another. If this happens, don't be afraid to return to your referral source for more names.

SPECIAL SERVICES FOR WOMEN. In many cities you can find a women's center that keeps a referral list of therapists. This may be a list of interested volunteer therapists, or it may be the result of a more thorough process of screening. Women's studies programs in colleges may also keep lists or have resources. Local chapters of the National Organization for Women usually try to maintain a referral list of particular interest to women. You could also check services such as rape crisis centers, shelters for battered women, or abortion/pregnancy counseling services.

FRIENDS. One of the best resources may be your friends. Ask about their experiences in therapy. Can they recommend names? Can they tell you whom to avoid? How did they evaluate their experience? Your friend's therapist might not be right for you, but s/he might be someone who could refer you to someone who is.

NEWSPAPER ADVERTISEMENTS. Another source of referrals is the local newspaper, especially one written for women or students. Newspapers sometimes have a referral list or carry ads from local therapists and clinics. Many professionals are up in arms about advertising, claiming that it is unethical, and while it is true that many people may advertise falsely, advertisements can nonetheless make you aware of the services that are available, especially those directed specifically to women.

CONSUMER DIRECTORIES. You may be able to find a local or regional directory prepared by a consumer group and carried in bookstores and libraries. In New England, for example, there is a *New England Women's Yellow Pages*. Directories like this can be a good place to start, but may be incomplete or out-of-date. They may also not have interviewed each person or group individually and may be working from second-hand information. Because a group puts out a referral list or even personally gives you a name does not mean unconditional endorsement of the person. You have to check it out yourself, and most groups would like feedback on any negative experiences that result from a referral.

Whatever route you follow to find a therapist, remember that no recommendation relieves you of the responsibility of deciding for yourself whether or not a therapist is right for you.

Types of Mental Health Services and How to Find Them

PRIVATE PRACTITIONERS. These are self-employed therapists from all backgrounds. They may be found in the *Yellow Pages* under different professional headings, such as Psychologist or Social Worker. They charge a fee for their services, and some may accept insurance payments.

FAMILY SERVICE AGENCY. These are found in the *Yellow Pages* under Social Services. They provide multiple services, often geared to a geographical area. They charge fees on a sliding scale, but may offer a free intake and referral.

CHILD GUIDANCE CLINIC. These offer services to children and parents when the child is experiencing difficulties in school or at home. They also charge fees based on a sliding scale.

COMMUNITY MENTAL HEALTH CENTER. They provide multiple services which may include day-treatment programs as a substitute for hospitalization, out-patient treatment for individuals, medication, referrals, educational programs. Usually no fee is charged, or there is a sliding scale. They may be connected with a state hospital.

STATE MENTAL HOSPITAL. This facility provides in-patient care for acute and long-term patients. It may have an out-patient clinic, especially for follow-up care. Payments are made on a sliding scale or through insurance.

PRIVATE PSYCHIATRIC HOSPITAL. In-patient psychiatric care is usually provided by the patient's own doctor, often on a short-term basis for acute problems. They charge standard hospital fees.

GENERAL HOSPITAL WITH PSYCHIATRIC WARD. These provide emergency hospitalization for acute problems and short-term hospitalization for patients of staff doctors. They may also have an out-patient clinic. They also charge standard hospital fees, with a sliding scale in the clinic.

VETERANS ADMINISTRATION HOSPITAL WITH PSYCHIATRIC WARD. They provide in-patient and out-patient care for qualified veterans. They can be located in the white pages of the phone book under United States Government, Veterans Administration.

COLLEGE COUNSELING SERVICE. This is available to students of that particular school only. They are usually free, but may provide a limited service or referrals only.

ALCOHOL OR DRUG ABUSE DETOXIFICATION CENTER AND/OR CLINIC. These provide multiple services for people with alcohol or drug-abuse problems. They are listed in the white pages for your state agencies, listed under the Department of Mental Health or the Department of Drug Abuse. Some centers may be maintained or connected with Alcoholics Anonymous, also to be found in the white pages.

CRISIS CENTER OR HOTLINE. These can be found in the *Yellow Pages* under Social Services or in advertisements in local papers. Some radio stations maintain lists of hotlines available to listeners. They usually offer short-term counseling for people in distress and referrals for long-term therapy. They may not charge any fee but usually ask for contributions.

Appendix B

Mental Patients' Bill of Rights

From *Your Rights as a Mental Patient in Massachusetts**

We do not think that abuses in hospitals can be eliminated by reforming the mental health system, any more than abuses under slavery could be eliminated by reforming slavery. Doing away with institutions that are inherently oppressive is the only way to abolish the wrongs of such institutions.

We do not romanticize what is commonly called "mental illness." We know that people can and do become angry, sad, frustrated and scared. We insist, however, that such people not be labeled ill, made into prisoners, and stripped of their rights and human worth because someone with more power and authority decides that the problem lies inside them (by reason of "mental illness") and not in the failures of society.

We think asylums are needed for people who become victims of society's failures. Such asylums must guarantee that people's fundamental human rights are not violated. The following rights are those we demand:

*Reprinted by permission of the Mental Patients Liberation Front, P.O. Box 89, West Somerville, Massachusetts 02144.

1. You have the right not to be locked up against your will.

2. You are entitled to protections theoretically guaranteed by the Constitution; this includes the right to notice and a hearing before being deprived of your freedom.

3. You have the right to an alternative to incarceration in a mental hospital or, should you want hospitalization, the right to decide which hospital you will be in.

4. You have the right to decent living conditions while in the hospital.

5. You have the right to a sexual life while in the hospital and the right to your sexual preference.

6. You have the right to uncensored communication by phone, letter, and in person with whomever you wish.

7. You have the right to use of phones free of charge. The phones should be available on every ward.

8. You have the right to keep your personal property; no one can confiscate what is legally yours.

9. You have the right to refuse to work in a mental hospital or to choose what work you shall do; you have the right to receive at least the minimum wage for such work.

10. You have the right to the integrity of your own mind and the integrity of your own body.

11. You have the right not to be subjected to physical abuse.

12. You have the right to adequate medical attention when you need it.

13. You have the right to have treatment and medication administered only with your consent, without coercion, and in full knowledge of their effects.

14. You have the right not to be used as a guinea pig for experimental drugs and treatments; you have the right to refuse to be anybody's learning material or, should you agree, the right to be paid for the use of your mind and body.

15. You have the right to the complete confidentiality of your records. You have the right to see your hospital records at any time.

16. You have the right not to have your character questioned or defamed whether in the hospital or afterwards.

17. You have the right to sue those who have mistreated you, and you are entitled to legal protection against retaliation by the hospital.

18. You have the right to patient-run facilities where the decisions that are made and work that is done are your responsibility and under your control.

Further, we think it is your right to keep and use this handbook, your right to get in touch with any of the Legal Aid Services listed at any time (even in seclusion and restraint or on a locked ward) and your right not to be punished for requesting this kind of assistance.

Recommended Readings

We particularly recommend the first six books as an introduction to the subject of women's special needs in therapy. We are also including the address of KNOW, Inc., a feminist press printing originals and reprints of books and articles at modest prices. They have several excellent selections on mental health.

KNOW, Inc.
P.O. Box 86031
Pittsburgh, Pennsylvania 15221

CHESLER, PHYLLIS. *Women and Madness.* Garden City: Doubleday, 1972.

GORNICK, VIVIAN, and MORAN, BARBARA, eds. *Women in Sexist Society.* New York: New American Library, 1971.

HENLEY, NANCY M. *Body Politics.* Englewood Cliffs, N.J.: Prentice Hall, 1977.

MILLER, JEAN BAKER. *Toward a New Psychology of Women.* Boston: Beacon Press, 1976.

SEATTLE–KING COUNTY N.O.W. *Woman, Assert Yourself.* New York: Perennial Library, 1976.

SMITH, DOROTHY, AND DAVID, SARA, eds. *Women Look at Psychiatry.* Vancouver: Press Gang Publishers, 1975.

ABBOTT, SIDNEY, and LOVE, BARBARA. *Sappho Was a Right-On Woman.* New York: Stein and Day, 1973.

ADLER, ALFRED. *Social Interest.* New York: Capricorn, 1964.

BARDWICK, JUDITH M. *Psychology of Women.* New York: Harper and Row, 1971.

BASSUK, ELLEN, AND SCHOONOVER, STEVEN. *The Practitioner's Guide to Psychoactive Drugs.* New York: Plenum, 1977.

BELLIVEAU, FRED, AND RICHTER, LIN. *Understanding Human Sexual Inadequacy.* New York: Bantam, 1970.

BERNARD, JESSE. *The Future of Marriage.* New York: World, 1972.

BERNE, ERIC. *What Do You Say After You Say Hello?* New York: Grove, 1972.

BOSTON WOMEN'S HEALTH BOOK COLLECTIVE. *Our Bodies, Ourselves.* New York: Simon and Schuster, 1971.

BINDER, VIRGINIA, ET AL. *Modern Therapies.* Englewood Cliffs, N.J.: Prentice Hall, 1976.

BROVERMAN, INGE K., ET AL. "Sex-Role Stereotypes and Clinical Judgements of Mental Health." *Journal of Consulting and Clinical Psychology* 34, No. 1, 1970.

CHAMBERLIN, JUDI. *On Our Own: Patient-Controlled Alternatives to the Mental Health System.* New York: Hawthorn, 1978.

CHODOROW, NANCY. *The Reproduction of Mothering.* Berkeley and Los Angeles: University of California Press, 1978.

CORSINI, RAYMOND, ED. *Current Psychotherapies.* Itasca, Illinois: F.E. Peacock, 1973.

DE BEAUVOIR, SIMONE. *The Second Sex.* New York: Alfred A. Knopf, 1952.

DELASZLO, VIOLET S., ED. *The Basic Writings of C.G. Jung.* New York: Modern Library, 1959.

DINNERSTEN, DOROTHY. *The Mermaid and the Minotaur.* New York: Harper and Row, 1976.

DREIFUS, CLAUDIA. *Woman's Fate.* New York: Bantam, 1973.

EHRENBERG, MIRIAM AND OTTO. *The Psychotherapy Maze.* New York: Holt, Rinehart and Winston, 1977.

EHRENREICH, BARBARA, AND ENGLISH, DEIRDRE. *Complaints and Disorders: The Sexual Politics of Sickness.* Old Westbury, New York: The Feminist Press, 1973.

ENNIS, BRUCE J. *Prisoners of Psychiatry.* New York: Avon, 1972.

FRANKS, VIOLET, AND BURTLE, VASANTI. *Women in Therapy.* New York: Brunner/Mazel, 1974.

FREEMAN, LUCY, AND ROY, JULIE. *Betrayal.* New York: Stein and Day, 1976.

FREUD, SIGMUND. *A General Introduction to Psychoanalysis.* New York: Pocket Books, 1953.

GOTKIN, JANET AND PAUL. *Too Much Anger, Too Many Tears.* New York: Quadrangle/The New York Times Book Co., 1975.

GREER, GERMAINE. *The Female Eunuch.* New York: Bantam, 1972.

HAMMER, SIGNE. *Daughters and Mothers/Mothers and Daughters.* New York: Quadrangle/The New York Times Book Co., 1975.

HEILBRUN, CAROLYN G. *Toward a Recognition of Androgyny.* New York: Harper and Row, 1973.

HIRSCH, SHERRY, ET AL, EDS. *Madness Network Reader.* San Francisco: Glide Publications, 1974.

HORNEY, KAREN, M.D. *Feminine Psychology.* New York: W.W. Norton, 1967.

JANOV, ARTHUR. *The Primal Scream.* New York: Dell, 1970.

JAY, KARLA, AND YOUNG, ALLEN, EDS. *Out of the Closets: Voices of Gay Liberation.* New York: Pyramid, 1972.

KAPLAN, BERT, ED. *The Inner World of Mental Illness.* New York: Harper and Row, 1964.

KAPLAN, HELEN SINGER. *The New Sex Therapy.* New York: Brunner/Mazel, 1974.

KIERNAN, THOMAS. *Shrinks, etc.* New York: Dial, 1974.

KLAICH, DOLORES. *Woman Plus Woman: Attitudes toward Lesbianism.* New York: Simon and Schuster, 1974.

KOEDT, ANN. *The Myth of the Vaginal Orgasm.* Somerville, Mass.: New England Free Press, 1970.

KOVEL, JOEL, *A Complete Guide to Therapy.* New York: Pantheon, 1976.

LOWEN, ALEXANDER. *Bioenergetics.* New York: Coward, McCann and Geoghegan, 1975.

LYONS, GRACIE. *Constructive Criticism.* Berkeley: Issues in Radical Therapy, 1976.

MACCOBY, ELEANOR EMMONS, AND JACKLIN, CAROL NAGY. *The Psychology of Sex Differences.* Stanford: Stanford University Press, 1974.

MANDER, ANICA VESEL, AND RUSH, ANNE KENT. *Feminism as Therapy.* New York: Random House, 1974.

MARTIN, DEL, AND LYON, PHYLLIS. *Lesbian/Woman.* San Francisco: Glide Publications, 1972.

MENTAL PATIENTS LIBERATION FRONT. *Your Rights as a Mental Patient in Massachusetts.* Somerville, Mass.: New England Free Press, 1975.

MILLER, JEAN BAKER, ED. *Psychoanalysis and Women.* New York: Brunner/Mazel, 1973.

MITCHELL, JULIET. *Psychoanalysis and Feminism.* New York: Random House, 1974.

MITFORD, JESSICA. *Kind and Usual Punishment.* New York: Random House, 1974.

MORGAN, ROBIN, ED. *Sisterhood Is Powerful.* New York: Random House, 1970.

PERLS, FREDERICK S. *Gestalt Therapy Verbatim.* Moab, Utah: Real People Press, 1969.

PIERCY, MARGE. *Woman on the Edge of Time.* New York: Alfred A. Knopf, 1976.

RAWLINGS, EDNA, AND CARTER, DIANE, EDS. *Psychotherapy for Women.* Springfield, Ill.: Charles C. Thomas, 1977.

REBETA-BURDITT, JOYCE. *The Cracker Factory.* New York: Bantam, 1978.

REICH, WILHELM. *The Sexual Revolution.* New York: Farrar, Straus and Giroux, 1945.

ROGERS, CARL. *On Becoming a Person.* Boston: Houghton Mifflin, 1961.

RUITENBEEK, HENDRIK M., ED. *Psychoanalysis and Female Sexuality.* New Haven: College and University Press, 1966.

RUSH, ANNE KENT. *Getting Clear: Body Work for Women.* New York: Random House, 1973.

SCHRAG, PETER. *Mind Control.* New York: Random House, 1978.

SHERFEY, MARY JANE. *The Nature and Evolution of Female Sexuality.* New York: Random House, 1966.

STEINER, CLAUDE. *Scripts People Live.* New York: Grove, 1974.

STROUSE, JEAN, ED. *Women and Analysis.* New York: Viking, 1974.

SZASZ, THOMAS. *The Myth of Psychotherapy.* Garden City: Doubleday, 1978.

————. *The Myth of Mental Illness.* New York: Harper and Row, 1974.

TENNOV, DOROTHY. *Psychotherapy: The Hazardous Cure.* Garden City: Doubleday, 1976.

THOMAS, SUSAN AMELIA. "Theory and Practice in Feminist Therapy." *Social Work* November, 1977.

WILLIAMS, ELIZABETH FRIAR. *Notes of a Feminist Therapist.* New York: Praeger, 1976.

WILLIAMS, JUANITA. *Psychology of Women: Behavior in a Biosocial Context.* New York: W.W. Norton, 1974.

WYCKOFF, HOGIE. *Solving Women's Problems.* New York: Grove, 1977.

Index